LIFEBOATS OF THE WORLD

LIFEBOATS OF THE WORLD
A Pocket Encyclopedia of
Sea Rescue

E. W. Middleton
Commander VRD, RNVR

ARCO PUBLISHING COMPANY, INC.
New York

Published 1978 by Arco Publishing Company, Inc.
219 Park Avenue South, New York, N.Y. 10003

Copyright © Blandford Press Ltd 1977

Printed in Great Britain

Library of Congress Cataloging in Publication Data

Middleton, Eric William.
  Lifeboats of the world.

  Includes index.
  1. Life-boats. 2. Lifeboat service. I. Title.
  VK473.M55   387.2   77–26247
  ISBN 0–668–04470–5
  ISBN 0–668–04481–0 pbk.

CONTENTS

ACKNOWLEDGEMENTS

As this book gives details of many different sea rescue organisations, it will be clear that the author must owe a great deal to a considerable number of people for much of the information that it contains. This is very much the case and so it is not possible here to mention by name all the individuals and organisations who gave such valuable assistance – but to all of them and to those anonymous benefactors in many organisations, the warmest thanks are extended.

The author's debt to the Royal National Lifeboat Institution will be obvious and he and the publisher are particularly grateful for permission to make use of some of the extensive records and for the facilities for doing so which were made by the Director, Captain Nigel Dixon. In addition a great deal of help, encouragement and advice was received from the Deputy Director, Mr John Atterton, Lieut-Commander W. L. G. Dutton, lately Chief Inspector of Lifeboats, and Mr Patrick Howarth, Public Relations Officer: Mr Alan Neal produced the answers to innumerable questions and Miss Joan Davies, Mr Andrew Gould and Mr Ray Kipling assisted and advised on the finding and selecting of illustrations.

Information and illustration material from abroad was not always easy to obtain and it was fortunate that the RNLI, as secretariat of the International Lifeboat Conference, had so much available. On the other hand, many countries and organisations responded generously and their help is very gratefully acknowledged. Several individuals very generously provided illustrations and information from their own personal records and in this category special thanks are due to Mr Grahame Farr (RNLI Honorary Archivist), Mr Cees van der Meulen (Heemsteede, Netherlands) and Mr Rob Anderson (Victoria, Australia).

In particular, tribute must be paid to the crews of the lifeboats of the RNLI and all the other sea rescue organisations throughout the world who have so often demonstrated the real meaning of self-sacrifice and of the brotherhood of man. To salute these men is the main purpose of this book.

FOREWORD

In Britain the lifeboat service enjoys the admiration and warm support of nearly everybody and it is only on rare occasions that much thought is given to the organisations of other countries. The fact that sea rescue arrangements can differ so widely and that there are so many types and designs of life-saving craft must come as a surprise to many people, including some closely involved in the lifeboat service in this country.

The many illustrations in colour, showing lifeboats and rescue cruisers from all over the world, vividly express man's ever increasing efforts to find the perfect craft. The details of the history of sea rescue in many countries leave no doubt of the general concern for the safety of those at sea.

As a lifeboatman who has experienced the dangers, difficulties and occasionally the frustrations of rescue work but also the joy of successful saving of lives, I am impressed with the way this book makes clear the unity of purpose and brotherhood of lifeboatmen the world over.

The chapter on lifeboat disasters makes sad but impressive reading and cannot but bring home the fact that however good the boat, it is on the men who man her that the distressed mariner must rely.

Commander Middleton was the inspector of lifeboats for the area when I first became coxswain and I know that he is well equipped to write on the wider aspects of sea rescue.

Richard Evans

ex-Coxswain Richard Evans, BEM,
of Moelfre, Anglesey.*

* Richard Evans is the only man living who has won two RNLI gold medals. He was also awarded the British Empire Medal for lifeboat services.

ILLUSTRATIONS

The author and publisher would like to express their grateful appreciation to all the organisations and individuals throughout the world who so kindly provided transparencies, photographs and illustration references for this book.

Credits for photographs reproduced:

Bermuda Search and Rescue Institute: pages 142, 143.
Board of Navigation and Maritime Affairs of the DDR: pages 171, 172 and Plates 70, 71
Brazilian Salvamar: page 188
Canadian Coast Guard: pages 137, 139, 140 and Plates 49, 50
Danish Administration of Navigation and Hydrography: page 163
Finnish Lifeboat Society: Plates 68, 69
French National Society for Sea Rescue: pages 174, 175, 177
Italian Ministry of the Merchant Marine: page 185 and Plate 84
Japan Lifeboat Institution: pages 206, 207 and Plates 87, 88, 89
National Sea Rescue Institute of South Africa: pages 192, 193
Norwegian Society for Rescue of the Shipwrecked: pages 153, 155, 156
'Observer': Plates 30, 101
Polish Ship Salvage Company: pages 201, 202
Portuguese Sea Recue Institute: page 182
Pressefoto Janssen/Schwenke: pages 168, 170
Royal National Lifeboat Institution: pages 113, 115, 212 and Plates 1, 2, 3, 4, 5, 9, 11, 12, 14, 17, 19, 20, 22, 23, 24, 25, 26, 27, 28, 29, 31, 32, 35, 56, 57, 72, 85, 98, 99

Spanish Red Cross of the Sea: pages 179, 180, 181
Sumner Lifeboat Institution Inc: pages 199, 200
Swedish Sea Rescue Society: pages 158, 159 and Plates 62, 64, 65
United States Coast Guard: pages 124, 128, 129, 130, 131, 132, 133, 135 and Plates 41, 42, 43
Valparaiso Lifeboat Volunteer Institution: page 189 and Plate 96
R. A. Anderson: pages 195, 196 and Plate 95
T. M. Carter: pages 111, 116, 235
Joan Davies: Plate 13, 36
G. Farr: Plates 10, 58, 63, 73, 74, 75, 78, 102
N. King: Plate 21
M. Tidy: Plates 15, 16, 97
D. Trotter: Plates 18, 33
C. van der Meulen: pages 144–149, 151 and Plates 51, 52, 53, 54, 55, 100

The RNLI craft illustrated in Plate 26 is an Oakley type, and not an Arun as stated in the caption.
The speed of the Spanish BM class vessel in the caption to Plate 81 should read 25 knots.

Other colour plates and line illustrations in the book were specially prepared by Clifford and Wendy Meadway/ Portman Artists.

INTRODUCTION

What may be considered the first conference of the sea rescue organisations of the world was held in London in June 1924 as part of the celebrations of the centenary of the founding in the UK of the Royal National Lifeboat Institution. Apart from the war years 1939–45, a conference has been held every four years since the inception, a different country acting as host on each occasion. In 1963 the turn of Great Britain to act as host had come round again and a highly successful conference was held in Edinburgh. This was attended by nineteen sea rescue organisations from various countries and a number of these sent their latest lifeboats to illustrate improvements in design and techniques.

At a number of these conferences the point was raised that there must be a number of countries with sea rescue organisations (about which little or no information was available) which did not attend the meetings. It was suggested that steps should be taken to fill the gaps in order to place on record a comprehensive description of all lifeboat and similar services – whether voluntary or state-run. Some progress was made, but it tended to be a slow process as a number of countries seemed reluctant to disclose details of their sea rescue arrangements. In some cases, this may have been due to the fact that sea rescue was included in the duties of the armed forces, and a possible breach of security was feared. In others, it is possible that there were no sea rescue arrangements and there was a natural reluctance to admit it but if there were such cases they must have been very few and far between. In any event, requests for information no doubt had to pass through 'the usual channels', some of which may have been clogged with the debris of awkward correspondence. Certainly there would appear to have been few instances of eager replies and there are still some long stretches of coastline which apparently have no rescue facilities of any sort, organised or otherwise. On the other hand it is possible that some of the sea areas involved do have some form of rescue craft or breeches buoy gear available and if so it is regretted that details were not forthcoming. However, each year more and more information comes to hand and details are given here of a number of organisations the existence of which has only come to light within recent months.

No attempt has been made to give full technical details of rescue craft mentioned as this would not conform to the intention of giving an easily assimilated overall picture of the sea rescue services of the world.

From the historical point of view it has only been possible to touch on the wider aspect of the development of the lifeboat and the organisation of rescue at sea and many names deserving of mention have had to be omitted. As far as Britain is concerned, there are several books which give comprehensive details of the history and development of the Royal National Lifeboat Institution. Other countries may not be so easy to research.

In 1974 the RNLI celebrated its 150th anniversary and an impressive lifeboat exhibition was held at Plymouth. Again, various nations sent examples of their rescue craft, pictures of which are included in the colour section of this book and which give some idea of the wide variety and impressive appearance of modern lifeboats.

THE COLOUR PLATES

1 Bamburgh Castle, Northumberland: where sea rescue began under the guidance of Archdeacon Sharp in 1786 with a coble of Lionel Lukin's design.

2 A wreck off the River Tyne in 1837 – from a painting by Stewart Henry Bell.

3 Model of the 'Original', Henry Greathead's first lifeboat. The curved or rockered keel was a feature of this design.

4 The lifeboat built to James Beeching's prize-winning design. After sea trials the boat was allocated to the Ramsgate station in Kent.

5   Launch from a horse-drawn carriage – from a painting by W. L. Wyllie. Justly famous
    for his fine marine paintings, the artist has immortalised the drama of a horse-drawn
    launch.

6   An early sailing lifeboat on her carriage.

7 The *James Stevens No. 3*, an early RNLI steam lifeboat. She was the first of her type to have screw propulsion as opposed to water jets.

8 One of the first RNLI motor lifeboats. She was stationed at Tynemouth and was 40 ft (12.19 m) long.

9　An RNLI Liverpool type lifeboat, 35½ ft (10.8 m) in length. A popular boat which at one time had almost completely ousted the self-righter.

10　Last launch of the RNLI Liverpool type lifeboat, Minehead, Somerset. This station now has an inflatable inshore lifeboat.

11   The RNLI 37 ft (11.3 m) Oakley self-righter lifeboat. This very able boat was designed to replace the 35½ ft (10.8 m) Liverpool type.

12   Another view of an Oakley lifeboat. The self-righting ability is obtained by transfer of water ballast.

13   Three stages of a typical launch by tractor of a lifeboat on a carriage.

Top left   The tractor moves boat from boathouse to launching place. For longer distances the tractor would tow the boat stern first.

Lower left   The tractor pushes boat on carriage into launching depth. This can be a difficult operation in heavy weather.

Above   The tractor moves back, hauling on the launching falls and launching the boat off the carriage. Close co-operation between coxswain and tractor driver is necessary to ensure launching at the right moment.

14 A typical RNLI station of the 19th century (Llandudno, N. Wales)

15 RNLI station with a slipway launch (Sennen Cove, Cornwall). Owing to the difficulties of the beach, this station has one slipway for launching and another for returning the boat to the house.

16 The RNLI lifeboat emerging on to the slipway at Sennen Cove station.

17 RNLI 37 ft (11.3 m) Rother class lifeboat. This is a modification of the original Oakley 37 ft type, and is provided with a wheelhouse.

18   RNLI 54 ft (16.45 m) Arun class lifeboat. Developed from the 52 ft Arun, this is a completely new RNLI type, fast and able.

19   RNLI 70 ft (21.3 m) Clyde class rescue cruiser. The only RNLI cruising type, which has comprehensive accommodation and fine sea-keeping qualities.

20 RNLI Yarmouth, Isle of Wight 48 ft (14.78 m) Oakley type lifeboat. Named *The Earl and Countess Howe* this was the first of the larger Oakley self-righters.

21 Ramsgate, Kent 47 ft (14.32 m) Watson type lifeboat in a rough sea. For many years the mainstay of the RNLI, this type was always popular with crews.

22　Capsizing trials of an RNLI Arun class lifeboat. (a) Commencement of the parbuckling of the boat by crane; this continues until the boat rests upside down on its cabin. The parbuckle or strop goes under the boat and is attached to the far gunwale.
(b)　Boat nearly capsized – sling about to be released.

(c) Boat righting herself.

(d) Boat righted and freeing herself of water.

23　St. Mary's, Scilly Isles, RNLI lifeboat at the rescue of the motor vessel *Braemar*.

24　RNLI McLachlan type $18\frac{1}{2}$ ft (5.6 m) inshore lifeboat.

25   RNLI Arun class lifeboat on the River Thames, passing the Houses of Parliament.

26 H.M. the Queen Elizabeth II on board the RNLI Arun class lifeboat *Royal British Legion Jubilee* after the naming ceremony at Henley-on-Thames.

27 RNLI 44 ft (13.4 m) Waveney class *Lady of Lancashire* at Fleetwood, Lancashire.

28 Schermuly line-throwing pistol about to be fired. This is used in conjunction with a breeches buoy when a lifeboat cannot get alongside a casualty.

29 A slipway launch at the Lizard – Cadgwith RNLI station in Cornwall.

30 A 21 ft (6.4 m) inflatable Atlantic type inshore lifeboat. This RNLI advanced design is very fast and seaworthy.

31 Inshore lifeboat building and repair shop, Cowes, Isle of Wight. Modifications and improvements in technique are under constant investigation by the RNLI.

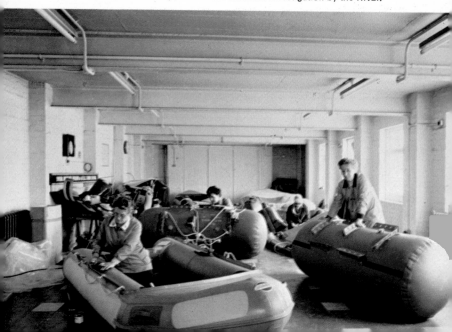

32 Launch of a RNLI inshore lifeboat. The ease and speed with which these handy craft can be launched is very impressive.

33 Inflatable RNLI inshore lifeboat at sea during trials. This picture gives some idea of the speed and manoeuvrability of these craft.

FINLAND

Suomen Meripelastusseura r.y.

USA

United States Coast Guard

FRANCE

Societe Nationale de Sauvetage en Mer

UK

Royal National Lifeboat Institution

NETHERLANDS

Koniklije Zuid-Hollandsche Maatschappij tot Redding van Schippbreukelingen

NORWAY

Norsk Selskab til Skipbrudnes Redning

SWEDEN

Svenska Sallskapet for Raddning af Skeppsbrutne

CANADA

Canadian Coast Guard

CHILE

Cuerpo de Voluntarios de los Botes Salvavidas de Valparaiso

SPAIN

Cruz Roja del Mar

34 Crests of some sea rescue organisations from around the world.

35 Display of lifeboats from around the world at the 1963 International Lifeboat Conference at Leith, Scotland.

36 International lifeboats at Plymouth for the RNLI 150th anniversary.

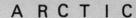

ARCTIC

NORTH
ATLANTIC
OCEAN

PACIFIC

SOUTH
ATLANTIC
OCEAN

The International Civil Aviation Organisation (ICAO), with
headquarters at Ottawa in Canada, publishes details of search
and rescue arrangements covering all the oceans of the world.
These facilities may be used for rescue of surface craft where no
other assistance is available.

PACIFIC
OCEAN

INDIAN
OCEAN

Members of the
International Lifeboat Conference

Countries not members of the I.L.C.
but known to have sea rescue facilities

Countries which may have sea rescue facilities
of which details have not been made
available to the I.L.C. In many cases, sea
rescue arrangements are in the hands of naval,
air-force and harbour authorities.

38   U.S. Coast Guard 378 ft (115.5 m) cutter *Chase* which operates from Boston, Mass. Fitted with the latest equipment and an 80 ft flight deck, she carries out long-range search and rescue patrols.

39 U.S. Coast Guard 44 ft (13.4 m) steel lifeboat. The RNLI Waveney class was developed from this design and a number of nations use versions of the design.

40   U.S. Coast Guard 41 ft (12.5 m) prototype utility boat capable of 24 knots and designed for search and rescue and law enforcement.

41   U.S. Coast Guard 44 ft (13.4 m) lifeboat negotiating heavy surf off the Umpqua river, Oregon. This boat once capsized in the surf but righted herself and continued operating.

42   U.S. Coast Guard 30 ft (9.1 m) lifeboat carrying out a rescue. A 44 ft lifeboat stands by in the background.

43 U.S. Coast Guard 30 ft (9.1 m) fibreglass utility boat from Rockaway lifeboat station, New York co-operating with a gas turbine HH52A helicopter from Brooklyn.

44 A boating safety detachment (BOSDET) of the 8th U.S. Coast Guard District on Lake Ponchartrain in Louisiana.

45   Bermuda Search and Rescue Institute jet propelled rescue craft, specially designed for work over coral reefs.

46   Canadian Coast Guard cutter *Daring*. With a length of 178 ft (54.25 m), this vessel is used primarily for search and rescue and has a speed of 16 knots.

47 Canadian Coast Guard cutter *Raleigh*. The lightweight inflatable can be seen stowed on board.

48 Canadian Coast Guard Atlantic rescue ship *Alert*. 234 ft (71.4 m) in length she has a speed of 18¾ knots and a crew of 38.

49   Canadian Coast Guard 44 ft (13.4 m) lifeboat at sea.

50   Canadian Coast Guard SRN5 Air/Sea rescue hovercraft landing a casualty.

51   Dutch (KZHRM) Atlantic class inshore lifeboat *Dolfijn* of the Bergsluis station.

52   Dutch (KZHRM) lifeboat *Javazee* from Breskens, at sea off the Isles of Zeeland.

53　Dutch (KNZHRM) lifeboat *Nicholas Marius*, from Terschelling, launched by tractor.

54　Dutch (KNZHRM) lifeboat *Dr Ir. S. L. Louwes* of the Zandvoort station, just returned from a rescue.

55   An exercise drill with the Dutch 'jumping net', used for rescue work, on the *Javazee* from Breskens.

56 Dutch (KNZHRM) lifeboat *Carlot* from the West-Terschelling station.

57 Dutch (KZHRM) lifeboat *Koningen Juliana* which operates from the Hook of Holland.

58 Norwegian rescue cruiser *Ambassador Bay* at Plymouth for RNLI 150th anniversary.

59 Norwegian rescue cruiser *Sjorfaren*. Length 28.4 m, speed 12 knots.

60 Norwegian rescue cruiser *Ada Waage* in ice conditions. Length 24.4 m, speed 12 knots.

61 Norwegian lifeboat *Ragni Berg*. Length 13.8 m, speed 20 knots.

62   Swedish inflatable type inshore lifeboat *Mariestad*.

63   Swedish rescue craft demonstrating the flotation net. During a rescue, survivors jump into the net from the casualty vessel.

64 Swedish rescue cruiser *Fritz Scheel* stationed at Halmstad-Grötvik. Length 14.5 m, speed 26 knots.

65 Swedish rescue boat *Gerda Hansson* and rescue cruiser *Dan Boström*.

66 Danish lifeboat MRB34 from Hvide Sande station on the west coast of Jutland. Length 15.10 m, speed 9 knots.

67 Danish lifeboat MRB35 stationed at Thyborøn on the west coast of Jutland. Length 15.1 m, speed $9\frac{1}{2}$ knots.

68 Finnish ice-breaker rescue cruiser *Wilhelm Wehlforss*. With a length of 68 ft (20.7 m) and built of steel, this is the rescue society's largest vessel.

69 Finnish lifeboat *Haapasaari*, built of wood in 1940's and reconditioned in 1975. Length 36 ft (11.0 m).

70   East German rescue cruiser *Stoltera*. Length 17.97 m and built in Poland in 1975.

71   East German mobile rocket launcher, used in conjunction with inflatable boats along
      the Baltic coast.

72   West German rescue cruiser *Arwed Emminghaus*. The 'daughter boat' is carried aft for use in shallow water.

73   West German cruiser *Georg Breusing* at Leith International Lifeboat Conference in 1963.

74 *Arwed Emminghaus* at Plymouth in 1974 for the RNLI 150th anniversary.

75 'Daughter boat' as stowed on a West German rescue cruiser. It is launched down the ramp through a door in the stern.

76 The latest German rescue cruiser *John T. Essberger,* fitted with a helicopter landing platform on the after deck.

77 Portuguese lifeboat *Nossa Senhora da Conceicão* stationed at Vila R. Santo Antonio.

78   French lifeboat *Pourquoi-pas ?* from St. Servan and at St. Malo for the 10th International Lifeboat Conference in 1967. Built in 1956 with a length of 13 m.

79   Fast French vedette type lifeboat *Anne de Bretagne* stationed on the Atlantic coast at Le Croisic.

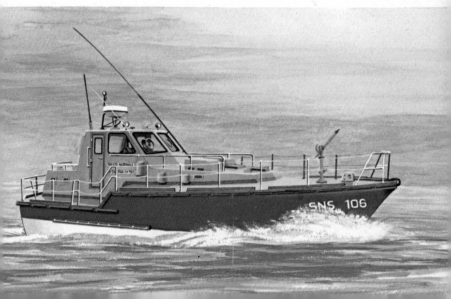

80 Spanish AA class lifeboat which operates in the Atlantic from Cantábrico. Length 15 m, speed 14 knots.

81 Spanish inshore lifeboat of BM class, used in Mediterranean from Malaga. Length 6 m, speed 9 knots.

82 Italian lifeboat of the Keith Nelson type. Length 40 ft (12.19 m), speed 21 knots.

83 Italian Boston whaler type fibreglass boat for coastal rescue work.

84   Italian Barnett type lifeboat CP301, built in the U.K. at Cowes, I.O.W.

85   Polish rescue cruiser *Monsun,* operating in the Baltic from one of the twelve rescue
      stations.

86   Polish rescue cruiser *Pasat.*

87 Japanese rescue cruiser *Skoyo*. Length 20.01 m, speed 10.6 knots.

88 Japanese *Nagoura Maru*. Length 19.5 m, speed 9.5 knots.

89   Japanese *Jintzu Maru*. Length 18.26 m, speed 11 knots.

90   A typical coastal rescue, showing the sequence of events:

1   The casualty ship calls for assistance by firing red rockets or flares; by making the international distress call sign SOS, by radio telegraphy, or the spoken word 'Mayday', by radio telephone. There are numerous other distress signals.
2   If the Coastguard lookout sights the casualty or receives the distress message, he will request that the lifeboat be launched, giving full details. If the casualty is close inshore, a coast rescue team with rocket apparatus and breeches buoy will proceed to the spot.

3 A member of the public sighting the casualty should telephone the emergency services and ask for the Coastguard. All details, especially of the position of the wreck, should be accurate.

4 According to the conditions and type of rescue involved, the inshore lifeboat, or

5 The offshore lifeboat would launch at once.

6 If necessary, the Coastguard would also request that a helicopter should assist.

7 If the position of the casualty were not known accurately an aircraft would carry out a search.

91 NSRI *St. Croix* lifeboat. Length 10 m.

92   South African NSRI lifeboat *John Roberts* based on Durban. Length 15 m.

93 Fibreglass rescue boat *Aid II* of the Sumner Lifeboat Institution of New Zealand. Length 15 ft (4.57 m).

95 (*Opposite*) Australian Watson type lifeboat, until recently stationed at Queenscliff, Victoria. 45 ft (13.7 m) long, she was built at Port Adelaide and went into service in 1926.

94 New Zealand 30 ft (9.1 m) self-righter *Rescue II* built in the U.K. at Cowes, I.O.W. Replaced by *Rescue III* by the Sumner Institution and now in service at Kaikoura.

96 The Valparaiso, Chile, lifeboat. A 46 ft (14 m) Watson type, she was bought from the RNLI in 1955.

97 Throughout the world, the work of rescue goes on. A lifeboat and crew put to sea once more on a rescue mission.

98   The lifeboat circles the casualty to assess the situation.

99   The crew having been taken off safely, the lifeboat leaves the sinking vessel.

100–102   However well designed and we
built a lifeboat may be, the succe
of a mission must always deper
on the skill, endurance and courag
of her crew.

Two typical members of lifebo
crews are shown here, one Dutc
(*top left*) and one British (*top right*
both born of seafaring nations ar
both dedicated to the work of se
rescue.

In a church in South Shields,
Tynemouth, the stained glass wi
dow (*left*) bears a silent witne
to the self-sacrifice and human
of the men of the lifeboat service

CHAPTER ONE

BRITAIN – THE CRADLE OF THE LIFEBOAT

Before the advent of canals and railways, the importance of coastal shipping was supreme. Transport of goods by road was slow, extremely expensive and quite impractical for some materials. At the same time coastal voyages were hazardous and no ship's master liked being in sight of the shore for longer than was absolutely necessary. Sea room was all important to sailing craft, as they were often at the mercy of sudden changes of wind direction and thousands of vessels were lost through becoming embayed on a lee shore, on to which they were mercilessly driven by gales and heavy seas. Not only coastal craft, but foreign-going vessels might end a voyage thus, sometimes almost as soon as it had begun.

Two classical examples of a number of ships driven ashore by a shift or violent increase of wind are often quoted. One took place in November 1703, when a hurricane drove a fleet of British ships on to the Goodwin Sands off the Kent coast. Many lives were lost but some hundreds of survivors got ashore on the sands and were in mortal danger from the rising tide. Appeals by the Mayor of Deal to local boatmen and the Revenue men to launch to their assistance met with blunt refusals. So the mayor and some fellow townsmen took the boats and gallantly put out to the rescue.

The other incident took place in Torbay, Devon, which was a favourite place for ships sheltering from the south-west gales. In January 1866, a large number of merchant ships of different nations had been waiting for better weather and some had sailed, only to return for shelter once more. During the night the wind increased in violence and gradually backed to the eastward, putting all the ships on a lee shore.

Some managed to get under way, a hazardous proceeding in the pitch dark with no room to manoeuvre, and soon many were ashore. In the morning the beaches were littered with ships and debris, including dead animals. The loss of life was grievous but many people were saved, mostly without help from the shore where onlookers could see and do little in the pitch darkness, strong wind and heavy surf.

Shipping losses in the eighteenth century, and indeed for most of the nineteenth century, were enormous. Of course, most of the vessels concerned were small coasters, many ill-found and with masters of dubious ability, although the general standard of seamanship was high. Hundreds of ships were lost each year and with them hundreds of seamen.

In view of the large sums of money involved in these disasters and the fact that the loss of trained seamen must eventually have proved a handicap to seaborne trade, it is surprising that it was not until the end of the eighteenth century that attempts were made to initiate some form of organised sea rescue. To some extent this may have been due to the fact that coast dwellers looked on a wreck as a gift from the gods and were said to have acquired a liking for all sorts of exotic beverages and expensive materials provided by the sea. For a long time, any sort of navigational aid like a lighthouse or beacon was frowned upon and there were many grim tales of ships actually being lured to destruction with false lights.

The birth of the lifeboat

The story of the lifeboat seems to have begun in 1772 at Bamburgh in Northumberland. Here, Dr John Sharp had succeeded to the living which included control of a trust set up by the Bishop of Durham, Baron Crewe. The trust supported a number of charities and Dr Sharp became concerned with the many wrecks occurring on this dangerous coast, doing what he could to warn and help vessels in trouble and look after survivors from those that came ashore.

Following these humane efforts, it would seem that the necessity for assistance to vessels in distress and for sea rescue generally began to be more widely appreciated. The names of the pioneers of lifeboat design are well known and their work recorded in some detail but today, to point to one man and say 'He was the inventor of the lifeboat' would be unwise, if not invidious. Chronologically, there is little doubt that the first name mentioned should be that of de Bernieres, a French official who designed and tested what appears to have been the forerunner of the self-righting lifeboat in 1775. But the craft was apparently not proposed for use as a rescue vessel and does not seem to have been put into service. Next comes Lionel Lukin, a fashionable coachbuilder with a lively, inventive mind. He patented what he called an 'unimmergible' boat in 1785 and in fact produced a rescue boat in 1786 for Dr Sharp at Bamburgh.

In 1789 the loss of the ship *Adventure* with all hands off South Shields, at the mouth of the river Tyne, led to a prize of two guineas (£2.10) being offered for the best design for a rescue boat to be placed at the river mouth. The initiative came from a club known as 'The Gentlemen of the Lawe House' and in spite of the smallness of the prize, a number of entries were received. Two of these came from men whose names will always be closely linked with the birth of the lifeboat – William Wouldhave and Henry Greathead. Their designs were considered the best but neither was held to warrant the award of the whole prize, which was divided between them. Wouldhave is said to have refused his guinea!

Eventually a design incorporating the best features with some modifications was produced, and from this Greathead built the 'Original' which was stationed on the Tyne and saved many lives over a period of forty years. At the time the boat and house cost £149. Today a new boat and house might well cost over a thousand times that amount.

Who then was the real inventor of the lifeboat? De Bernières, Lukin, Wouldhave or Greathead? All may share in the honour and indeed there is plenty to share. Apart from the self-righting* quality which both de Bernières and Wouldhave introduced as original ideas, the main feature of the early lifeboats was the provision of adequate buoyancy to the extent of making the boats virtually unsinkable. Hundreds of individual buoyancy cases are still one of the characteristics of a lifeboat today.

The beginnings of organisation

This then was the position in Great Britain in 1823 when, possibly influenced by the recent disaster to HMS *Racehorse* on Langness, a southern point of the Isle of Man, Sir William Hillary who lived in Douglas published a pamphlet appealing for the formation of a national institution for the preservation of life from shipwreck. He pointed out that the existing arrangements were unco-ordinated and left long stretches of coastline unprotected.

Hillary's appeal met with a sympathetic reception and two members of parliament, George Hibbert and Thomas Wilson, gave him active support. As a result of their efforts, a public meeting was held in the London Tavern on 4 March 1824 with the Archbishop of Canterbury in the chair. From this meeting the 'National Institution for the Preservation of Life from Shipwreck' was formed with Mr Thomas Wilson as chairman of the committee. The Earl of Liverpool was president and King George IV agreed to become patron. The ubiquitous Captain Manby, inventor of the line-throwing mortar, also attended the meeting.

The Shipwreck Institution got off to a good start and received £10,000 in donations in its first year. Twelve new lifeboats were placed on the coast to supplement some thirty-nine already existing. The number of lives saved in 1824–25 was recorded as 342, so it must be conceded that the effort was well worth while.

*Throughout this chapter, the description 'self-righter' applies to boats with inherent righting qualities and *not* to the modern versions in which the righting moment is achieved by transfer of water ballast or some other specially contrived means. These latter are discussed later in the book.

Although Greathead's boats were still in favour, two other designers produced new types which became popular. One was Pellew Plenty of Newbury in Berkshire, who also built the boats, and the other was George Palmer, at one time commander of an East Indiaman and for some years deputy chairman of the Institution. Plenty's boat was described as of the Norfolk wherry type with a broad beam and Palmer's as similar to a whale boat, double-ended with a rounded section and narrow beam.

Unfortunately, the initial momentum of the Shipwreck Institution was not maintained as a period of great distress and hardship throughout the country set in. From 1828 when the Earl of Liverpool died until 1851 when the Duke of Northumberland accepted office, the Institution was without a president. Funds, and public enthusiasm for the service were very low indeed but a welcome if somewhat protracted change of fortune had in fact begun.

In 1850, Richard Lewis became secretary of the Shipwreck Institution and served it well until he died thirty-three years later. The Duke of Northumberland, himself an admiral, infused new life into the direction of affairs and also offered a prize of a hundred guineas for the best design for an improved lifeboat. In the matter of funds things were not quite so happy and in 1854 a number of significant changes took place. First, the name was altered to the 'Royal National Life-boat Institution for the Preservation of Life from Shipwreck' and the care of shipwrecked persons was made the responsibility of the 'Shipwrecked Mariners' Benevolent Society'. Further, a subsidy from the government in the form of a grant of £2,000 a year from the Mercantile Marine fund was accepted and this entailed the observance of certain conditions. This grant saw the RNLI through a difficult period of reconstruction until 1869 when it was decided that this support was no longer necessary. From that time onwards the whole of the required finance for the lifeboat service has been forthcoming from voluntary contributions.

The transition from sail to steam

For nearly a hundred years after the advent of the first sea rescue organisation in Britain, lifeboats were dependent on oars and sails for motive power.

Even so, the increasing use of steam propulsion posed new problems for the rescue services and eventually altered the character of casualties to a considerable extent. The steamer, providing her engines were serviceable, was far less vulnerable to the effects of a sudden onshore wind than sailing craft and major disasters such as those which happened in Torbay and the Downs, became a matter of history. In the early days of steam there were many casualties due to inefficiency of engines and boilers and even in the present day, engine failure is still a fairly regular cause of calls for assistance, if not of actual wreck. But on balance, the change to steam power was favourable in that the number of casualties was reduced and less lives were lost.

Pulling and sailing lifeboats continued to deal with all ship casualties and a large steamer in difficulties was still dependent on sail for succour. To survivors anxiously awaiting rescue, the sight of the sturdy little lifeboat driven by a scrap of sail must have caused mixed emotions and the mechanically minded must have considered the possibility of a better way of doing things. But it is a matter of some certainty that the lifeboatmen themselves were as one man in rejecting any such new-fangled notions.

Thus it was that in spite of the rapid mechanisation of industry during the nineteenth century the lifeboats really altered very little. The competition sponsored by the Duke of Northumberland when he became president of the RNLI and which offered a prize of one hundred guineas for the design of an improved lifeboat had a good response. Two hundred and eighty models were submitted, many of which were ingenious and some really merited the overworked description 'fantastic'. The prize was awarded to James Beeching of Great Yarmouth for a design of the whale-boat type, 36 ft long with a beam of $9\frac{1}{2}$ ft.* She was a self-righter and carried a dipping lug and mizen sails. A cork fender, air cases and twelve relieving valves were fitted and she pulled twelve oars, double-banked.

Amongst the many designs submitted was a lifeboat driven by a steam engine, the idea of a Mr G. Remington of Warkworth in Northumberland. This boat was 40 ft long, screw propelled and had a 10 hp engine. There is no doubt that this was one of the earliest proposals for a steam-driven lifeboat, but not the first. In fact, it was some thirty-six years later that the RNLI made any definite move towards the adoption of steam power for lifeboat propulsion. One reason for the delay was some doubt on the part of the committee of management as to the practicability of a coal-fired boiler in a small boat in heavy weather, and as to the possibility of getting a mechanically-minded crew; particularly in view of the active aversion to the idea on the part of lifeboatmen. At places where steam tugs were available, these were used to tow the lifeboat when necessary and crews frequently expressed preference for this method as against steam propulsion for the boat itself. Possibly because they felt that at the end of a tow rope they were much safer than in close proximity to the infernal machine.

Certainly, in the early days of steam, there were sufficient disasters due to engine or, more often, boiler failure to convince the sceptical seaman that he was safer with sail. An historic example of disaster due to the failure of mechanical propulsion has been perpetuated in the story of Grace Darling.

The *Forfarshire* was a paddle steamer of some 300 tons and was bound from Hull to Dundee in September 1838. While at Hull, a leaking boiler was repaired but further boiler trouble occurred off Flamborough Head next day and with a strong north-west wind the ship made little headway. With night coming on, the wind shifted to east-of-north and just as

*Throughout this book, dimensions are quoted as found in the relevant historical account.

it had been decided to set the auxiliary sails she carried, the engines failed completely.

Driven at the mercy of the gale the ship began to approach the land and not long afterwards the *Forfarshire* struck a rock near the Longstone lighthouse and almost at once broke in two, drowning many of those on board. Grace Darling's father was the keeper of the Longstone lighthouse and the gallant rescue carried out by the father and daughter has been described again and again. Grace herself survived the incident by no more than four years. She died at the age of twenty-six.

The boiler failures which brought about the end of the *Forfarshire* with the loss of most of her crew and passengers were not uncommon in those days, and indeed for some considerable time afterwards. Steam pressures were very low, which was probably just as well, but it is easy to appreciate the feelings of lifeboatmen that such things might make uncomfortable shipmates.

James Beeching's lifeboat did not find full favour with the RNLI and a modified design was built at Woolwich dockyard under the supervision of James Peake, a member of the committee of management. This also embodied the self-righting principle and from these two designs sprang a long line of self-righters with various other modifications. Peake's boat was 30 ft in length and had six relieving tubes to free the boat of water.

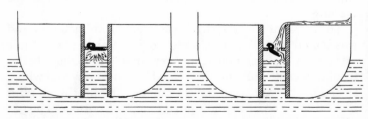

Simplified diagram of the relieving valves used to remove through the bottom of the boat any water taken on board.

This system of taking water out through the bottom of the boat often causes some surprise to laymen, although, in fact, it is quite simple. The tubes are fitted with a non-return valve which prevents water coming up into the boat but allows any water in the boat to flow down, at least to the level of the sea outside. Normally, these valves will clear the boat completely as she lifts in a seaway. In decked boats, scuppers in the side (also generally fitted with non-return flaps) allow excess water to flow overboard. Freeing the boat of water taken on board as quickly as possible is all important, as loose water moving from side to side is a great enemy of stability.

Launchings

Probably one of the most difficult problems is getting a lifeboat afloat. In the early days, with comparatively light pulling and sailing boats this was fairly easy, with the boat on a carriage and horses for motive power if necessary. Many of the horses used became familiar with the launching procedure and were said to gallop to the gates of their fields on hearing the maroons calling out the lifeboat. One old-stager died in his tracks as the lifeboat launched off her carriage into the wintry sea, just as old lifeboatmen, relegated to launching duties, have done in their time.

Not all beaches were suitable for launching off a carriage,

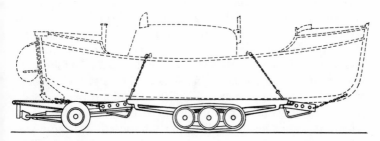

Diagram of the type of carriage used to transport lifeboats over roads and flat beaches, showing the method of securing the boat to the carriage.

and with larger boats this ceased to be practical anyway. Where the boat could lie afloat in a harbour, there were few problems, but in many places it was necessary to build a house with a slipway for the boat to launch down. These were sometimes necessary on exposed coasts, and in this case re-housing at the end of a service might be impossible in bad weather, so that the boat had to go to the nearest harbour. Indeed, round the coasts may be found a wide variety of methods of getting a lifeboat away to sea in all weathers. Launching and recovering a lifeboat can be extremely hazardous and calls for great skill and judgement on the part of the coxswain and launching party.

Equipment

All the gear in a lifeboat was, and of course still is, of the finest quality obtainable and of a strength amply sufficient to withstand the severe conditions likely to be experienced. This meant that in the sailing boats the gear was very heavy and needed strong arms to handle it. All these boats had big iron drop keels, which could be released quickly if they became jammed or entangled in wreckage. The solid masts and heavy tanned sails needed considerable effort to hoist them, but once up they would stand a wild blow without flinching. The equipment, other than that needed for pro-pulsion, was simple in the extreme, the most important item apart from the compass being the drogue. A lifeboat's drogue is a cone-shaped bag of heavy canvas open at both ends, with strong strops and about three feet in diameter at the towing end, tapering to rather less than a foot at the other. The wider end is kept open by a strong wooden hoop. In following seas the drogue is towed astern attached by a swivel to some twenty fathoms of manila rope, with a smaller rope made fast to the trailing end for hauling the drogue back on board when no longer necessary. Properly handled, a drogue will allow the boat to run with heavy breaking seas astern of her without fear of broaching-to. There is little doubt that even today the drogue is an essential piece of equipment for a lifeboat and it is possible that more than one disaster might have been averted had the drogue been running properly. Drogue handling requires great care and a small mistake

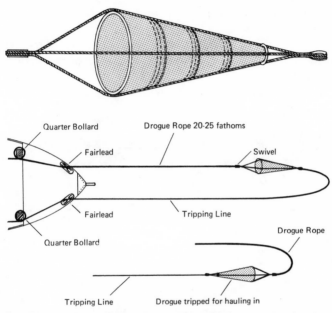

Construction and operation of lifeboat drogue. In the larger drogues, wire strops and metal hoops are used.

may result in the tripping line, as the hauling-in rope is called, fouling the drogue-towing rope, with the result that the two become entwined and lay up into one solid length. The drogue will then neither run properly nor can it be hauled in, creating a very nasty situation in a heavy sea.

Life-belts for the crew, heaving lines, a simplified breeches buoy arrangement, flares, some provisions and water completed the equipment other than that commonly carried in boats. Nevertheless, a sailing lifeboat with all her gear stowed looked rather like a mobile ship chandler's and there was little room to move about until the masts were up and the sails hoisted. Survivors would be stowed wherever possible and in the eyes of a survivor comfort is a small matter compared with safety.

Design developments
The self-righter
The story of the development of the lifeboat is one of trial and error, ingenuity and wishful thinking, courage, deter-

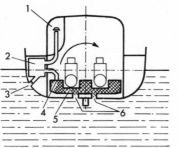

Boat in normal trim.

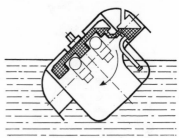

Boat capsizing to starboard.

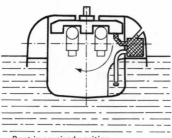

Boat in capsized position.

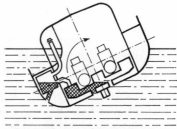

Boat continues turning to starboard through 360 degrees and resumes normal position.

Self-righting principles of the Oakley type lifeboat; capsize to starboard.

Water ballast is contained in a tank (5) in the bottom of the boat to which the water is admitted through sea inlets (6) which close in the capsized position as does the air intake.

As the boat turns over the water runs from the ballast tank to a righting tank on the port side (2).

mination and stubbornness. In fact, a small mirror of life itself. The latter half of the nineteenth century was the era of the self-righter both in Britain and abroad, though by no means all lifeboatmen were convinced of its superiority. Richard Lewis, secretary of the RNLI from 1850 until his death in 1883, was the champion of this type and in his book *The Life-boat and its Work*, published in 1874, he made his

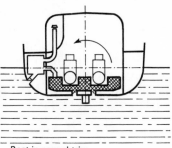

Boat in normal trim.

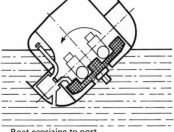

Boat capsizing to port.

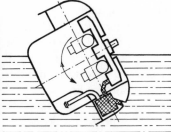

Boats turning moment is checked.

Boat returns to normal position in the reverse direction having turned through 180 degrees.

Self-righting principle of the Oakley lifeboat; capsize to port. The filling of the righting tank checks the roll to port and returns the boat to the upright position by making her roll back to starboard.

This transfer of weight to one side puts the boat out of balance and makes her continue turning until nearly upright when the water flows back from the righting tank into the ballast tank again. The whole operation is controlled by specially designed valves (3 and 4) which open or close at the correct moment.

preference very clear. He also laid down the essential qualities for a lifeboat as 'extra buoyancy, self-bailing, ballasting, self-righting, stability, speed, storage room and strength'. Over a period of some twenty years from 1852 the records showed that there had been thirty-five capsizes of self-righting boats with the loss of twenty-five lives out of 401 people on board. In the same period eight lifeboats which were not self-righters capsized with the loss of 87 lives out of 140. As most of the boats in service were self-righters even the proportion of capsizes was in their favour. This may be considered somewhat surprising, as the self-righter of those days, with its comparatively narrow beam and high end-boxes, almost certainly had less initial stability. Over the years, this type of self-righter gradually lost favour until eventually only a handful remained on the coast. They were not easy boats to handle and it is possible that it was only the consummate skill of the coxswains that kept their reputation high.

The standing of the self-righter was considerably affected by a major disaster in 1886 when two lifeboats were lost with all but two hands, making it the worst tragedy in the history of the RNLI and possibly in the history of lifeboats up to the present day. The story demands a place in any record of lifeboats and lifeboatmen, apart from the effects the disaster had upon the design and operation of future boats.

The barque *Mexico* of Hamburg, outward bound from Liverpool to Guayaquil, went aground on the banks at the mouth of the river Ribble off Southport, Lancashire, on the night of 9 December 1886. There was a full gale blowing from the south-west and the vessel had apparently failed to make an offing, and been gradually driven down to leeward until she struck in the shallows extending for miles on either side of the mouth of the Ribble. Her distress signals were seen, the Southport lifeboat crew assembled and, pulled on her carriage by a team of horses the lifeboat was taken nearly four miles along the sands and launched to windward of the stricken vessel. The whole area was a mass of broken water, but the lifeboat managed to reach the *Mexico* with what must have been a superhuman effort on the part of the oarsmen. Off the starboard bow of the casualty, the coxswain gave orders for the anchor of the lifeboat to be let go, with the intention of veering down on the wreck. At this moment a towering breaker burst upon the lifeboat and capsized her in a flash. Thirteen of the crew were drowned but two stalwarts clung to the boat and came ashore with her safely.

Meanwhile, the St Anne's lifeboat, stationed on the north side of the Ribble mouth had launched through heavy surf with some difficulty. Nothing more was seen or heard of her that night and next morning the boat was found on the beach, bottom up. There were no survivors.

The Lytham lifeboat, stationed in the river Ribble, also launched and in heavy seas and pitch darkness, found the barque *Mexico* and rescued her crew of twelve, all of whom had lashed themselves in the rigging.

That night 27 lifeboatmen lost their lives. They left 16 widows and 50 fatherless children.

This terrible disaster had no effect whatever on the behaviour of other lifeboat crews. New boats to replace those lost were immediately forthcoming and so were men to man them – a splendid lifeboat tradition. But there was as might be expected a considerable outcry and demands to know how and why it happened. The main result of the full investigation was a revision of the specification and design of subsequent self-righters, the inference being that the self-righting power of the boats lost had not been sufficient.

But the ability to self-right is not necessarily the greatest safety factor in a lifeboat and if it were it would not be unreasonable to expect working boats to be given similar ability. In heavy weather, men thrown out of the boat as she went over and righted might well be unable to get back on board – and this has actually happened in more than one instance. In fact, the new self-righters built as a result of the investigation into the Southport disasters were given less beam, higher end-boxes and a heavier iron keel. It is probable that they were not very comfortable boats in very rough seas and needed expert handling. The lifeboats without self-righting properties had more beam and were less likely to capsize in the first place, but if they did capsize men might be trapped underneath them. This has happened in several disasters. So the decision as to which type was the best was a difficult one. The final choice, of course, always remained with the crews. In 1910 there were 182 self-righters in the RNLI fleet and 99 lifeboats without self-righting ability.

Another far-reaching consequence of the Southport disaster was the appointment by the committee of management of the RNLI of a consulting naval architect. The man chosen was G. L. Watson and he made an outstanding contribution to lifeboat design which has lasted right down to the present day. He was also a very successful designer of yachts, the famous *Britannia* and *Shamrock II* amongst many others.

G. L. Watson had reservations about the self-righting principle and suggested that although it might be wise to retain it in the design of pulling boats it should be possible to produce better sailing lifeboats without it. The result was the Watson sailing lifeboat which proved his point and was the forerunner of a long line of splendidly seaworthy and handy craft. It is possibly a coincidence but in the same year that Watson became consulting naval architect to the RNLI it was decided to explore further the suggestion for a steam-driven lifeboat.

Steam-powered lifeboats

The record says that a model of a steam lifeboat was submitted to the RNLI by the firm of R. and H. Green of Blackwall, London, who were given the order to build a prototype. This vessel, 50 ft long with a beam of 14 ft 4 in, had a draught of 3ft 3 in, which seems remarkably little for her size and the fact that she had to accommodate an engine and boiler, as well as fuel! The answer may be the fact that she was jet-propelled. The engine drove a very powerful pump which sucked in water and discharged it through tubes, the force of the ejected water driving the boat along. Although this system got over the problems of the screw racing in heavy weather, and the possibility of it being fouled or damaged by wreckage, there are some conflicting reports as to its efficiency. These seem to be borne out by the fact that later models were given screw propulsion. Nevertheless the *Duke of Northumberland*, as the first steam lifeboat was named, remained in service for thirty-three years and rescued 295 lives. On completion in 1890, she was sent to the RNLI Harwich station and she subsequently saw service at Holyhead and New Brighton.

In all, six steam lifeboats were built for the RNLI and one at least for an overseas service. Of these, following the *Duke of Northumberland* came the *City of Glasgow* in 1894, the *Queen* in 1897, *James Stevens No. 3* about 1898, *James Stevens No. 4* in 1899 and another *City of Glasgow* in 1901. In 1900, *James Stevens No. 4*, the Padstow, Cornwall, lifeboat capsized on service with the loss of eight of her crew and the following year a boiler explosion in the *Duke of Northumberland* killed her two firemen. The last steam lifeboat was withdrawn from service in 1928.

In view of the difficulty of obtaining trained men locally to maintain and operate the machinery and boilers of the steam boats, the engineroom staff were employed full time. Very little imagination is required to visualise the conditions below decks in the tiny engineroom and boiler room when the lifeboat was at sea in heavy weather. Battened down below and flung about by the violent motion of the boat, not only must firing have been a difficult and dangerous task but the strongest of stomachs must have been necessary. Strange as it may seem to the landlubber, lifeboatmen do get seasick occasionally which makes their courage all the more remarkable. It needs a lot of character to be brave *and* seasick. At one lifeboat station the honorary secretary reported that he kept a little canvas bag in which he put the false teeth of members of the crew before they embarked, as on one occasion several men lost theirs over the side!

But before this, in December 1900, the *Duke of North-umberland* carried out a splendid double service, rescuing the crews of two vessels. In a strong south-west gale she went to the assistance of the White Star liner *Cufic* off the Skerries rocks and succeeded in saving forty-one persons. There was a second lifeboat stationed with her at Holyhead at the time and on her return the crew of the *Duke of Northumberland* learned that this other boat had been out to a vessel in distress but had lost her anchor (probably in veering down to the casualty) and had to return for another one. So the steam lifeboat put out again after midnight and rescued the crew of the schooner *Julia* of Gloucester in the most severe conditions she had ever encountered. This rigorous winter service lasted ten hours in the most testing conditions and must have gone a long way to prove the ability of Britain's first steam lifeboat and also, it would seem, her water jet propulsion.

Tugs
Up to the time of the mechanisation of the boats themselves, tugs were quite frequently employed to tow them to the vicinity of the casualty. These tugs were hired locally for the purpose and their skippers and crews must have been exceptionally brave, able seamen. The service of the Ramsgate, Kent, lifeboat in January, 1881 to the sailing ship *Indian Chief*, aground on the Long Sand in the Thames estuary in a heavy gale of wind, was reported in the *Daily Telegraph* newspaper in what must be one of the finest and most moving pieces of sea literature ever written. The lifeboat was towed out to the Long Sand from Ramsgate by the tug *Vulcan* and the report, mostly in the words of the indomitable coxswain, Charles Fish, vividly conveys the discomforts and dangers of the undertaking. Certainly, it is clear that the men in the tug shared both with the lifeboatmen and were equally deserving of admiration and praise. Possibly some day the story of the partnership of tugs and lifeboats on rescue missions will be told, but up to now it has been a neglected study.

Some details of the developments in the other rescue services of the world are given in the appropriate chapters elsewhere in this book, but many countries, the European nations in particular, made use of the experience and efforts of Britain. Germany, for instance, had a number of boats of Peake's design and the self-righter type was widely used in various forms.

The coming of motor lifeboats

As with steam, the committee of management of the RNLI did not immediately succumb to the attractions of the internal combustion engine, no doubt for similar reasons. In dealing with lifeboat crews, the motto 'hasten slowly' has usually proved wise, though the tempo might fairly be said to have speeded up somewhat in the latter half of this century. Although in the case of steam, a boat was designed and built to accommodate the engine and boiler, this was not so with the first petrol engine installed, an existing lifeboat being modified to take it. This was in 1904 and after trials lasting about a year the first motor lifeboat so designed in Britain was laid down. She was completed in 1908 and allocated to Stromness in Orkney, a second motor lifeboat being completed in 1909 for nearby Stronsay. In April of that year, the two motor lifeboats in company with a sailing lifeboat for Thurso in Caithness, Scotland, left London for their stations where they arrived after a successful voyage lasting seventeen days, having made demonstration calls at a number of lifeboat stations on their way.

In the early motor lifeboats, the engines were considered auxiliary to the sails and were by no means as powerful as would be considered necessary today. The four cylinder Tylor engine, which developed from 40 to 50 hp was in favour and Tylor engines were used in lifeboats for many years. In the USA the fitting of what was there known as the gasolene engine proceeded more rapidly, as might perhaps be expected. By the time Britain had 13 boats fitted with motors, out of a fleet of 283, the USA had already motorised half their fleet which numbered approximately the same.

Thus, the coming of the internal combustion engine signalled the end of the steam lifeboat and if new designs or improvements were considered they did not get further than the drawing board. So while many active brains were engaged in exploring the possibility of producing the perfect lifeboat, the men who took lifeboats to sea were by no means easy to convince that any new-fangled design was going to be safer or more simple to handle than the craft they had been born and bred to.

Conclusions

Many people find it difficult to understand how a lifeboat can still be overwhelmed by the sea and lost with all hands. Surely, they say, modern technology can produce a boat which is safe in any weather. Up to the present this has not proved possible, for a variety of reasons. Enormous forces are generated by storm conditions and to add to the difficulties of lifeboat design, the boats *must* be able to operate in shallow water, for that is where most casualties occur. Shallow draft is also essential for launching purposes except where a boat is in a deep water harbour and these stations are few and far between.

So, in order that she may be able to meet the demands made upon her, a lifeboat must be a compromise between what the designer would like to do and what he must do. For the rest, everything must depend on the skill and courage of the men who man her.

CHAPTER TWO

THE CHANGING PATTERN – THE POST-WAR RNLI

The building of lifeboats in Great Britain was at a standstill for nearly the whole period of World War II. New designs were planned and considered, but not a plank was adzed until victory was clearly in sight. There was a lot of leeway to make up and in 1945 a considerable building programme had been initiated by the RNLI. At Cowes, on the Isle of Wight, the shipyards of Groves and Gutteridge and J. Samuel White had laid down the keels of a number of lifeboats, the majority of them being the 35 ft 6 in Liverpool type, now built with an increased beam of 10 ft 8 in and with twin screws. Suitable small diesel engines were not available for the earlier boats of this class, but they were fitted as soon as possible. Larger boats were also being laid down in increasing numbers, the policy being to replace all single screw craft as soon as practicable.

Not only were new boats an urgent requirement but men also. Most of the RNLI's inspectors of lifeboats were recalled to service in the Royal Navy in 1939, only two remaining on the coast to help ensure that the rescue service continued to function. They were assisted by retired inspectors who willingly returned to duty. At the end of the war, two inspectors had reached retiring age so new men were engaged to replace them. In addition, many coxswains of lifeboats had carried on for the war period regardless of age and some had topped the seventy mark. The same thing applied to many crew members so replacements for the grand old men had to be recruited from the returning servicemen. There was no lack of volunteers.

Most of the district engineers and hull surveyors had

remained with the RNLI during the war years and so were conversant with the state of affairs on the coast in 1945. The inspectors, new and old, had to find out for themselves and this entailed visiting every lifeboat station under their control as soon as possible and organising crew and committee meetings at most of them. As motor cars were at a premium most of the travelling had to be done by train and bus with quite a bit of foot-slogging as well, for lifeboat stations tend to be in most inaccessible places. Carrying a change of clothes, oilskins, seaboots and all the necessary files and paperwork in all weathers; taking boat after boat to sea on exercise and occasionally on service, often in bitter winter conditions, some inspectors must undoubtedly have wondered what on earth there is about the sea that makes a man seek such a living. Cars have made life easier but in general conditions on the coast are much the same today in the lifeboat service.

The many new boats under construction were all earmarked to replace old ones, and as soon as they had run their trials, they sailed for selected lifeboat stations. On this occasion, the RNLI's district inspector would be in command and the coxswain, mechanic and two hands from the station would accompany him as crew. This gave the crew a chance to get used to the new boat and her equipment on the voyage so that they would be quite at home in her and ready to take her out on arrival if necessary. Many of the passages were long – and in winter they could be very arduous. It was usual to put into harbour each night, as at that time, none of the lifeboats had any sleeping accommodation, but it was the practice to make at least one night passage. This enabled all lights and other night equipment to receive a proper trial. More facetiously it was said that it was also done to confirm that the inspector could find his way about in the dark! Possibly this stems from some of the stories of passages in the early motor lifeboats when the less reliable engines led to some hair-raising incidents and great hardship for the crews. On one occasion, a small lifeboat ended one winter day voyage of stopping, starting and drifting by grounding on a lee shore in the middle of the night. The inspector, who was suffering from a raging toothache, climbed a formidable cliff to get help – and incidentally find out where they were.

Technical aids

The immediate post-war pattern of boat construction and reorganisation of stations has been mentioned briefly. It may be assumed that the planners envisaged similar life-saving requirements to those obtaining before the war. In fact, this proved not to be the case. During World War II, there had been many excellent inventions, a number of which applied to navigation and safety at sea. Radar enabled the seaman to see in fog or in the dark. From another wartime invention, the Decca navigator was produced, automatically recording a ship's position in certain areas with minute accuracy. Echo sounders gave the depth of water with speed and efficiency, and direction-finding equipment was easy to operate in conjunction with the many radio beacons around the coast. In addition, the technique of damage control evolved under combat conditions had minimised the danger of a ship becoming a total loss. It really seemed almost impossible for a ship to get into difficulties through faulty navigation and indeed not so many did as in the past. But some still managed to do so and radar managed to achieve the unenviable reputation of 'assisting collisions'. An expert on the subject of collisions recently suggested that the figure for those occurring in the English Channel was so high that it must be close to the random expectation. In other words, nearly as high as it would be if no effort was made to avoid collision at all!

New accident areas

Nevertheless the professional seaman seemed to be keeping out of trouble, at least to a greater degree than in the first half of the century, but a new candidate for sea rescue appeared on the scene in ever-increasing numbers – the yachtsman.

Either because of the number of people who got sea experience during the war, or the crowded state of the roads as more and more cars became available, or just because of the sea in their blood, more and more people throughout the world turned to the sea for recreation and relaxation. A great upsurge in water sports took place as people settled down to a comparatively peaceful existence, which even the frequent eruption of bigger and better experimental atomic bombs seemed unlikely to interrupt. Sailing, in tiny dinghies or ocean racers; motor boating and cruising with little outboards or huge diesel engines; angling, nearly the oldest of pastimes; water ski-ing and skin diving, even ordinary swimming, attracted thousands of new adherents, to the benefit of their health and pleasure.

As the number of yachting and boating casualties steadily increased, this aspect of the RNLI rescue work came more and more into the public eye. It had a small but significant effect on fund raising, as a number of supporters felt that saving people who went to sea for their own amusement, and particularly the salvage of their vessels, was not exactly what the people in the street gave their money for. The reply of the experienced yachtsmen was that *they* were not the ones who made calls on the rescue services but rather it was the people who carried unsuitable dinghies on the tops of their cars and launched them all over the place with no idea of the risks they were taking. In fact, the statistics showed that this was not so and that a great number of calls were to yachtsmen who had fairly considerable experience. The reason being that with greater experience the tendency was to make longer trips and to be less inclined to insist on a good weather forecast in order to do so. The sea being what it is, this invariably leads to having to deal with really bad weather at some time or other. Bad weather places increasingly greater stresses, not only on the vessel and her gear but on the crew also, so that everything tends towards a situation in which trouble if not disaster can come quickly and unexpectedly. It does not need an actuary to predict that the number of casualties will rise in something like direct proportion to the increasing number of units at risk.

Another change in the general rescue situation also became clear in the immediate post-war period. This was that the conventional lifeboat as employed by the RNLI, sturdily built to the highest possible specification and powered for long trips in heavy seas, was not at all suitable for rescuing bathers, dinghy sailors and exotic amusement craft like pedalos. Ex-government rubber dinghies, airbeds and other floating paraphernalia also gave rise to calls for the lifeboat, often in a flat calm sea. In many cases, these calls ended in frustration for the lifeboat crew who would arrive on the scene to find that a speedboat running trips in the bay had been alerted and had done the job already!

Helicopters
Another wartime development was the helicopter, already in use for air–sea rescue work and soon to become involved in helping unfortunate swimmers, dinghy sailors and vessels of all sorts and sizes. This particular aspect of sea rescue met with an enthusiastic reception and in some quarters was hailed as the beginning of the end for lifeboats. Time, in fact, proved otherwise.

Co-ordination of rescue services in Britain
Of course, it became necessary to co-ordinate the rescue services, but before going into the details of this somewhat complex organisation, it is necessary to explain the rather casual-seeming connection between the RNLI and the Coastguard service in Britain. Although quite separate organisations, one a completely unfettered, charitable institution, the other a state-controlled body, the two together are really *one* rescue service. The RNLI provides everything necessary for the actual operations at sea, and the Coastguards undertake all the duties on shore. These include the provision of look-outs, co-ordination and communication arrangements and also rescue from the shore by

rocket line and breeches buoy. This last device has been the means of saving many lives and improved propellants and

Lifeboat Station

Inshore Lifeboat Station during summer only

Inshore Lifeboat Station all year round

rockets have extended the range of contact very considerably of recent years. The Coastguard have developed highly efficient drills and techniques and have carried out many difficult rescues involving tremendous efforts by the coast rescue teams. The unofficial link between the Coastguard and the RNLI represents a typical British compromise which has worked efficiently and in an atmosphere of friendly association and occasional mild rivalry over a long period.

Local RNLI organisation

Local control of a lifeboat is in the hands of the honorary

Type and location of sea rescue facilities in Britain:

1 Aith (Shetland); 2 Lerwick (Shetland); 3 Stromness (Orkney); 4 Kirkwall (Orkney); 5 Longhope (Orkney); 6 Thurso; 7 Wick; 8 Invergordon; 9 Buckie; 10 Macduff; 11 Peterhead; 12 Aberdeen; 13 Stonehaven; 14 Montrose; 15 Arbroath; 16 Broughty Ferry; 17 Anstruther; 18 Kinghorn; 19 Queensferry; 20 North Berwick; 21 Dunbar; 22 St Abbs; 23 Eyemouth; 24 Berwick-upon-Tweed; 25 North Sunderland; 26 Craster; 27 Amble; 28 Newbiggin; 29 Blyth; 30 Cullercoats; 31 Tynemouth; 32 Sunderland; 33 Seaham; 34 Crimdon Dene; 35 Hartlepool; 36 Teesmouth; 37 Redcar; 38 Runswick; 39 Whitby; 40 Scarborough; 41 Filey; 42 Flamborough; 43 Bridlington; 44 Whithernsea; 45 Humber; 46 Humber Mouth (Cleethorpes); 47 Mablethorpe; 48 Skegness; 49 Wells; 50 Sheringham; 51 Cromer; 52 Happisburgh; 53 Great Yarmouth & Gorleston; 54 Lowestoft; 55 Southwold; 56 Aldeburgh; 57 Harwich; 58 Walton & Frinton; 59 Clacton-on-Sea; 60 West Mersea; 61 Burnham-on-Crouch; 62 Southend-on-Sea; 63 Sheerness; 64 Whitstable; 65 Margate; 66 Ramsgate; 67 Walmer; 68 Dover; 69 Littlestone-on-Sea; 70 Dungeness; 71 Rye Harbour; 72 Hastings; 73 Eastbourne; 74 Newhaven; 75 Brighton; 76 Shoreham; 77 Littlehampton; 78 Selsey; 79 Hayling Island; 80 Eastney; 81 Calshot; 82 Lymington; 83 Bembridge (IOW); 84 Yarmouth (IOW); 85 Mudeford; 86 Poole; 87 Swanage; 88 Weymouth; 89 St Peter Port (Guernsey); 90 St Helier (Jersey), St Catherines (Jersey); 91 Lyme Regis; 92 Exmouth; 93 Torbay; 94 Salcombe; 95 Plymouth; 96 Fowey; 97 Falmouth; 98 Coverack; 99 The Lizard; 100 Penlee; 101 St Mary's (Scilly Isles); 102 Sennen Cove; 103 St Ives; 104 St Agnes; 105 Newquay; 106 Padstow; 107 Port Isaac; 108 Bude; 109 Clovelly (Cruising); 110 Appledore; 111 Ilfracombe; 112 Minehead; 113 Weston-super-Mare; 114 Barry Dock; 115 St Donats; 116 Porthcawl; 117 Port Talbot; 118 Mumbles (Swansea); 119 Horton & Port Eynon; 120 Bury Port; 121 Tenby; 122 Angle; 123 Little & Broadhaven; 124 St David's; 125 Fishguard; 126 Cardigan; 127 New Quay; 128 Aberystwyth; 129 Borth; 130 Aberdovey; 131 Barmouth; 132 Criccieth; 133 Pwllheli; 134 Abersoch; 135 Porthdinllaen; 136 Trearddur Bay; 137 Holyhead; 138 Moelfre; 139 Beaumaris; 140 Conway; 141 Llandudno; 142 Rhyl; 143 Flint; 144 West Kirkby; 145 Hoylake; 146 New Brighton; 147 Lytham St Anne's; 148 Blackpool; 149 Fleetwood; 150 Morecombe; 151 Barrow; 152 St Bees; 153 Workington; 154 Silloth; 155 Kippford; 156 Kirkudbright; 157 Portpatrick; 158 Stranraer; 159 Girvan; 160 Troon; 161 Largs; 162 Helensburgh; 163 Tighnabruaich; 164 Lamlash (Arran); 165 Campbeltown; 166 Islay; 167 Oban; 168 Mallaig; 169 Barra Island; 170 Stornoway; 171 Lochinver; 172 Arranmore; 173 Portrush; 174 Red Bay; 175 Bangor; 176 Donaghadee; 177 Cloughey-Portavogie; 178 Newcastle; 179 Clogher Head; 180 Howth; 181 Dun Laoghaire; 182 Wicklow; 183 Arklow; 184 Rosslare Harbour; 185 Kilmore; 186 Dunmore East; 187 Tramore; 188 Youghal; 189 Ballycotton; 190 Courtmaesherry Harbour; 191 Baltimore; 192 Valentia; 193 Galway Bay; 194 Ramsay (IOM); 195 Douglas (IOM); 196 Port St Mary (IOM); 197 Port Erin (IOM); 198 Peel (IOM).

secretary of the RNLI station branch. He is in fact the executive officer on the spot and other than in exceptional circumstances has complete authority to say whether a boat is to launch or not. He is advised but not ordered by the Coastguard and of course normally consults his coxswain. He need not have sea experience and possibly the majority of honorary secretaries have not been professional seamen, but living by the sea and amongst the men who man the lifeboat it would be quite wrong to belittle their ability. The standard is very high and all these hardworking, unpaid officials take tremendous pride in their job and in their boat and crew but there is perhaps still a tendency for a station to work as a unit rather than part of a team. Immediately following criticisms the RNLI took steps to improve co-ordination which, it must be said, had shown little sign of failure in the past.

Air–sea rescue

The air–sea rescue arrangements for the UK are co-ordinated by the Maritime Headquarters Rescue Co-ordination Centres (MHQ/RCC) at Plymouth and Pitrearie, near Edinburgh. Any request for major air assistance is dealt with by these two commands and for sea rescue the application would normally be made by the Coastguard. The use of helicopters has already been considered but when the search of large sea areas is necessary the assistance of fixed wing aircraft becomes essential. This is an expensive business, far more so than the deployment of a helicopter which is costly enough. On more than one occasion, after an extensive search by aircraft at enormous expense to the taxpayer, the vessel they were seeking has been found to be safe in harbour all the time. The moral is that you should keep *somebody* informed as to where you really are.

The lesson of a disaster

Few sea disasters have made such an impact on the general public as the loss of the car ferry *Princess Victoria* in 1955. Barely six years old, she was one of the first purpose-built car ferries put into service in Britain and was considered a very able vessel for the thirty-six mile sea crossing from Stranraer in Scotland to Larne in Northern Ireland. On 31 January, when she sailed on her normal ferry run, the weather was appalling with gales and high seas. Soon after leaving Loch Ryan, a heavy sea damaged the doors of the car deck which soon flooded. Later more big seas crashed on board giving the ship a list and rendering her virtually out of control.

Two hours after sailing, *Princess Victoria* asked for the assistance of a tug by radio. An SOS was broadcast an hour later when a position was given still close to the entrance to Loch Ryan. In fact, this position appears to have been considerably in error and she was really some miles to the south-west and well out in the Irish Sea. The Portpatrick lifeboat, which had launched at once on receiving the SOS, could find no trace of the vessel in or about the position given and other vessels including a destroyer joined in the search without success.

Then came an ominous message from the stricken ship that the coast of Ireland was in sight and that preparations were being made to abandon ship. The Donaghadee lifeboat, stationed just south of Belfast lough, launched immediately and proceeded to a position where survivors had been sighted but when she arrived the ship had foundered. For four hours the disabled vessel had been drifting across the Irish sea and had very nearly completed the crossing. The lifeboats rescued 33 people but of the 179 passengers and crew, only 43 survived.

It seems incredible that a modern vessel on a ferry run could not be found for four hours, even in bad visibility, in such narrow waters and that she sank before help could arrive. As a result of the subsequent inquiry there was a complete review of rescue organisation and a general determination to ensure that such a thing could not happen again.

Neither of the lifeboats concerned in this rescue was, at that time, fitted with direction-finding equipment, but new boats were being fitted and the value of this method of finding a casualty was fully realised. Its value was not always fully appreciated by lifeboat crews, in particular the older men who had not had war-time experience of its capabilities. In one case a boat which had been at sea a long time went many miles out of her way because the coxswain flatly refused to believe that the bearing his mechanic had obtained by DF was correct.

Not many lifeboats were fitted with radio telephones in 1945, but all new boats had modern sets installed and older boats were fitted as the equipment became available. Echo sounders came somewhat later and it must be appreciated that a lifeboat is a very small vessel and a great deal of her space being taken up with the twin tunnels in which the propellers work, in older designs, and by the great number of air cases which give additional floatation. The fitting of additional equipment always poses problems, not only of space but of weight, as it is vitally necessary to keep weight as low in the boat as possible to preserve stability. Every new piece of equipment which was suggested undoubtedly brought headaches to the lifeboat designers and builders. When, in due course, radar was available in a size that made it a practical proposition in a lifeboat, its weight and the space required led to a lot of hard thinking and reassessment of values. The decision to press on and fit all this complicated equipment was undoubtedly correct, but not easy to make. There must obviously be a limit to the space that may be given to equipment at the expense of room for survivors. Every new item added to the complications of proper maintenance and there was always the question of whether the crews would become sufficiently interested and train to become proficient with the instruments, so as to justify the very substantial amount they added to the cost of a lifeboat. A cost which was already escalating at a dizzy rate.

Other post-war changes

All these post-war problems affected other nations as well as Britain in greater or lesser degree. In the USA particularly, the rescue problems due to the enormous expansion of yachting and boating were tackled with typical thoroughness and expertise by the US Coast Guard. All owners of craft used for recreational purposes were encouraged to turn to their local Coast Guard unit for help and advice. A great deal of instructional literature was issued freely and a numbering system, obligatory for all vessels with engines of more than ten horsepower, introduced. The laws regarding pleasure craft varied from state to state but followed a similar pattern and were enforced by the Coast Guard who also laid down equipment requirements, inspected and approved the gear and issued instructions on safety afloat and the handling of craft. All these conditions, with perhaps some modifications, apply today. In addition, a civil penalty may be imposed by the Coast Guard for failure to comply with numbering requirements, failure to report a boating accident and so on. The approach to recreational seafaring varies in other countries but none appears to have instituted such careful control as the United States. In Britain the view of the majority of amateur seamen seems to be quite bluntly that they would rather lose their lives than the liberty to risk them. However, some sort of control, particularly of high speed craft, would appear to be inevitable some time in the future.

RNLI 37 ft (11.28 m) Oakley type lifeboat in rough weather off the harbour at Bridlington.

For the RNLI, the major post-war innovation due to the ever-increasing need for quick rescue in summer was the introduction of the inshore lifeboat. This was an inflatable dinghy, about 15 ft long and powered by an outboard motor giving a speed of up to 24 knots. The first few boats of this type did not reach their selected stations on the coast until 1963, but similar craft had been in use elsewhere for some years. The ILB, as this class is known, quickly became very popular and proved extremely effective; improved versions followed. According to recent figures ILBs saved more lives in 1970 than did the conventional lifeboats. This possibly supports the theory that you have only got to establish a lifeboat somewhere and the casualties will appear. Certainly by far the greater number of casualties occur in the immediate vicinity of the lifeboat stations and it would be unwise to assume that this is entirely due to clever siting.

In 1976 the active fleet of the RNLI consisted of 134 lifeboats and 123 inshore lifeboats as shown in the table.

Type	Dimensions	Number
Clyde	70 ft (21.3 m)	2
Arun	52 ft, 54 ft (15.8–16.4 m)	3
Barnett	52 ft (15.8 m)	14
Solent	48½ ft (14.8 m)	10
Oakley	48 ft (14.6 m)	5
Watson	46 ft to 47 ft (14.0–14.3 m)	39
Waveney	44 ft (13.4 m)	12
Watson	41 ft, 42 ft (12.5–12.8 m)	10
Beach	41 ft, 42 ft (12.5–12.8 m)	3
Keith Nelson GRP	40 ft (12.2 m)	1
Rother	37½ ft (11.4 m)	6
Oakley	37 ft (11.3 m)	22
Liverpool	35 ft (10.8 m)	6
Thames	50 ft (15.2 m)	1
Inshore lifeboats inflatable	15½ ft (4.7 m)	97
Inshore lifeboats	21 ft (6.4 m)	17
Inshore lifeboats	18 ft (5.6 m)	7
Inshore lifeboats	17 ft (5.2 m)	2
Total		257

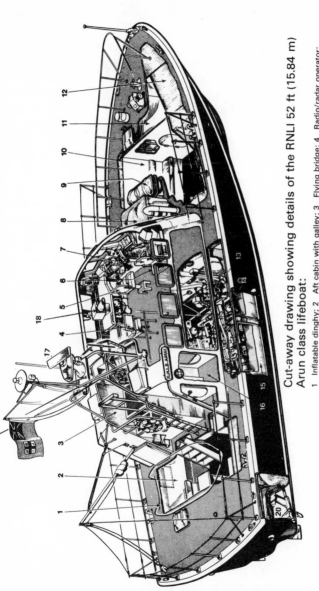

Cut-away drawing showing details of the RNLI 52 ft (15.84 m) Arun class lifeboat:

1 Inflatable dinghy; 2 Aft cabin with galley; 3 Flying bridge; 4 Radio/radar operator; 5 Coxswain; 6 Watertight hatch to forward cabin; 7 Navigator; 8 Rope stowage; 9 Emergency life-raft; 10 Forward cabin; 11 Cable locker; 12 Polyurethane foam buoyancy; 13 Petter generator set; 14 2×375 shp 'Caterpillar' D336 diesel engines; 15 Fuel tanks with 259 gallons (port and starboard); 16 'Coffer dam' entrance to wheelhouse (prevents flooding if boat capsizes); 17 Radar scanner; 18 Radar display unit; 19 Whip aerial; 20 Starboard propeller.

During 1975 the RNLI lifeboats answered 2,876 calls for assistance and saved 1,038 lives. On 28 May 1975 the Institution recorded the 100,000th life saved since its foundation in 1824. Thirteen medals for gallantry were awarded that year, three silver and ten bronze.

The RNLI building programme for 1976 consisted of 13 offshore lifeboats as follows:

> 50 ft (15.2 m) Thames class (1)
> 44 ft (13.4 m) Waveney class (5)
> $37\frac{1}{2}$ ft (11.4 m) Rother class (3)
> 54 ft (16.4 m) Arun class (4)

In addition, there were 52 lifeboats of various types in the reserve fleet, principally employed in relieving station boats for refitting.

The new boats

The appearance of the 37 ft Oakley in 1958 with self-righting ability obtained by transfer of water ballast and subsequently the application of the same principle in the $48\frac{1}{2}$ ft class was the first in a series of major changes in RNLI design. The return to self-righters, which had almost disappeared from the fleet, was dictated by a number of post-war capsizes in which members of the crew were trapped underneath the boats. Ironically enough, they were probably drowned by their life-belts, which would make it difficult and nearly impossible to submerge far enough to escape from under the boat. Even today, a quick release for life-belts might be valuable. The RNLI has decided that all new boats must self-right and that all non self-righters in the fleet must be converted by 1980. In some cases, this will be done by fitting air bags which will inflate automatically if the boat heels past the point of normal self-return. Transfer of water ballast has been abandoned in later boats and the self-righting achieved mainly by the buoyancy of superstructure. Up to the time of writing none of the new generation of self-righters has capsized on service or exercise so

Cut-away drawing showing details of the RNLI 44 ft (13.4 m) Waveney class lifeboat:

1 Fairlead; 2 Bollard; 3 Emergency tiller cap; 4 Steering gear; 5 Locker seat; 6 Stern floodlight; 7 Grab rail; 8 Stokes stretcher; 9 Main engines; 10 5-gallon foam cans; 11 Water-tight doors (quick acting); 12 Exhaust outlet; 13 Exhaust silencer; 14 Towing bollard; 15 Breeches buoy; 16 Steering transmission; 17 Console; 18 Compass; 19 Radar display unit; 20 Coxswain's seat; 21 Engine room ventilator; 22 Ship's bell; 23 Stern light; 24 Searchlight; 25 Towing light; 26 UHF dipole aerial; 27 Masthead light; 28 Radar scanner; 29 Windscreen wiper (straight-line type); 30 Danforth anchor; 31 Chemical toilet; 32 Radio telephone; 33 Lifting eyeplate; 34 Whip aerial; 35 Boat hook; 36 Water-tight hatch; 37 Echo sounder; 38 Hydraulic windlass; 39 Stemhead fairlead and jack staff socket; 40 Anchor light.

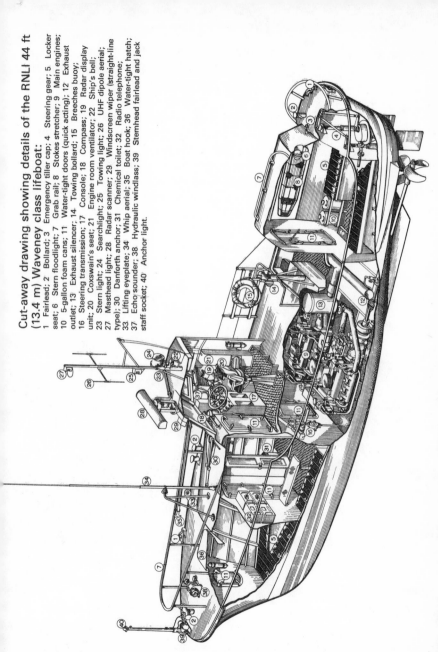

that the life-saving value of this ability has yet to be proved. All self-righters are capsized deliberately during building trials.

The building of the two 70 ft steel rescue cruisers followed a visit of RNLI officials to the Netherlands and Germany, when vessels of this type were examined and admired. These fine craft have a speed of $11\frac{1}{2}$ knots and draw 9 ft, which severely limits their capabilities for inshore work. They carry an inflatable boat on deck and have good accommodation for a crew of five to live on board.

RNLI Waveney class lifeboat returning to harbour at Whitby.

Great interest in the new US Coast Guard steel 44 ft lifeboat was expressed by delegates to the International Lifeboat Conference in Edinburgh in 1963, and the RNLI was able to purchase one for evaluation under European conditions. Such a marked difference in design evoked some early criticism but their speed of 13 knots, ease of manoeuvring and excellent equipment and accommodation, together with considerable towing ability, found favour with many crews. Six boats to a slightly modified design were built at Brooke Marine, Lowestoft and subsequently another eight boats with further modifications were ordered. This class cannot be used on slipways and has to lie afloat. The US Coast Guard now have over 100 of the 44 ft lifeboats.

A 40 ft glass re-inforced plastic (GRP) lifeboat was built for evaluation using a standard commercial hull and this craft was stationed at Calshot in Hampshire. A switch to steel construction for the $48\frac{1}{2}$ ft Oakley boats was made in the hope that this would materially decrease the cost but in fact the result was a saving of no more than 10 per cent.

The latest production has been the 52 ft Arun class, which has a draught of $4\frac{3}{4}$ ft and a speed of 20 knots. This rather revolutionary concept visualised a fast lifeboat, fully self-righting and with heavy weather capability. The design was by G. L. Watson & Co. of Glasgow, whose founder and his successors have been so closely associated with the RNLI and many successful lifeboats. The prototype was built of cold moulded ply by William Osborne Ltd. of Littlehampton and she has cruised to Spain and Scandinavia.

CHAPTER THREE

THE USA, CANADA AND CARIBBEAN

When we consider the beginnings of sea rescue in North America, we find conditions very different from those described so far. For a start there is a much longer coastline, which, in the eighteenth century, was sparsely populated and with great stretches virtually uninhabited. Shipping was comparatively scanty and many parts of the coast hardly ever saw a sail, so that the need for life saving arrangements was not brought home as drastically as on the crowded coastal waters, say, of the eastern sea shore of England. At the same time, there was a similar requirement for the carriage of goods by sea, with an even greater lack of suitable roads and even greater distances between communities, making shore transport slow and costly, if not impossible. The ports were busy and grew rapidly, and it is likely that good seamen were soon in short supply, a fact which would add to the urgency of suitable rescue facilities at known danger spots. The main difficulty with such a long, indented coastline would be to decide which were the main danger areas and how best to deploy the facilities available.

The USA

During the period immediately prior to the first recorded efforts at organised sea rescue in Britain, the American War of Independence was being fought. Certainly, on the American side, there can have been little time or effort available for anything but the vigorous prosecution of the war, until it was successfully concluded and the treaty signed in 1783. During the war, the number of American ships increased considerably and the seaborne trade and search for markets expanded rapidly with the coming of peace. It may be remembered that Nelson's determination to uphold the navigation acts in the West Indies brought him into conflict with the local authorities and the masters of American ships, some of whom instituted legal proceedings against him, one claim being for £40,000. This was but one indication of the vigorous and extensive sea trade which undoubtedly led to the need for organised rescue arrangements on the coast.

The first organisations
At the time Archdeacon Sharp was preparing the first lifeboat station in Britain at Bamburgh, the Humane Society of Massachusetts was formed, eleven years after the founding of the Royal Humane Society in Britain. It seems likely that there was some connection between these two events. Both societies had as their main object the prevention of death by drowning. In Britain at the time, there was some popular prejudice against attempting to revive a person who had stopped breathing and it took some time to overcome this. In fact, in one way and another, the shipwrecked mariner might be considered to have had only an outside chance of survival.

In 1789, the Massachusetts society began to establish shelters on the coast for the relief of survivors from shipwreck who managed to reach the shore, for it had been found that in the past many had perished from exposure on uninhabited stretches. In 1807, the first lifeboat was provided and stationed at Cohasset by the society. This boat was manned by a volunteer crew. The society was not well provided with funds and although other boats were built and stationed on the coast over the next few years there was insufficient money to maintain them properly.

Not all the seafaring activities of the time were concerned with legitimate trading and it soon became necessary for the new government to take steps to deal with the rapid increase in the popular pastime of smuggling. This had been considered a respectable occupation before and during the War of

Independence but now that the revenue from taxes was going into different coffers the situation had changed completely. In 1790, Alexander Hamilton, Secretary of the US Treasury, came to the conclusion that unless smuggling was stopped the young nation would soon be in dire financial straits and asked Congress for funds to build ten cutters with which to enforce the law. Thus the Revenue Marine came into being and grew in importance and prestige, through all the vicissitudes and growing pains of a new nation.

In 1831, another duty was added to the responsibilities of this versatile force when the revenue cutters were instructed to aid seafarers and ships in distress and were later charged with preventing the plundering of wrecks. It would appear that this latter occupation, like smuggling, was popular on both sides of the Atlantic.

Secretary of the Treasury John Spencer reorganised the Revenue Marine in 1843 as a bureau within his department somewhat on the lines of that obtaining with the Coast Guard today. At about this time the service began building cutters with iron hulls and auxiliary steam power. Some of these proved defective and were scrapped or converted. One reason for this was probably the new and untried method of propulsion by a completely submerged paddle-wheel. The primitive boilers and lack of efficient safety valves must have made these early steamships distinctly hazardous vessels in which to serve. However, the enterprising outlook which produced them can be taken as typical of the US Coast Guard attitude throughout its adventurous existence.

Meanwhile the Massachusetts Humane Society continued its efforts to save lives from shipwreck and drowning and in 1849 Congress provided the collector of customs at Boston with $5,000 to buy boat-houses and equipment for them. But it was considered that the voluntary arrangements were inadequate and Congress shortly afterwards voted $10,000 to build government lifeboat stations on the coast of New Jersey and to provide 'surfboats, rockets, carronades and other apparatus for the better preservation of life and property from shipwrecks on the coast'. To begin with all these stations were manned by volunteers and in the following year similar arrangements were made for the Long Island coast; but lack of properly organised supervision soon began to make itself felt and much of the equipment was eventually found to be unfit for use.

A number of wrecks occurred in 1854 and 300 lives were lost off the New Jersey coast, bringing home to the people on shore the need for proper rescue facilities if the seafaring trade was to be maintained. As a result, paid supervision of the lifeboat stations was arranged and also some payment to the crews, who were only engaged for three winter months. These shore-based stations and the revenue craft afloat provided the sea rescue facilities up to the year 1871 when Sumner Kimball, chief of the Revenue Cutter Bureau, put in hand steps to reorganise completely the life saving side of the service which was reported to be in bad shape.

He took immediate steps to remedy the defects. He secured an appropriation of $20,000 from Congress and overhauled the whole organisation. Proper crews were appointed and unsuitable men relieved of their duties. New boats and gear were provided and new stations established, together with a system of regular patrols. As a result, the loss of life on the coast was drastically reduced. The US Life Saving Service had been firmly established.

Even so, the financial situation was by no means easy and the majority of stations were operational in winter only, and that from the beginning of December each year. In 1877, two disasters followed one another within months, bringing home once more the necessity for still better rescue arrangements. In November, the steamship *Huron* drove ashore on the coast of North Carolina with the loss of 98 lives and three months later the *Metropolis* went ashore on Currituck beach. In the latter case a hundred people were saved by line-throwing apparatus but 85 lost their lives. As a result it was decided to establish a further thirteen stations between Cape Henry and Hatteras inlet but a great hurricane in October

1878 delayed the work and seriously damaged many existing sites.

About this time, a new bill was passed by Congress, again reorganising the rescue service, its control and management. The life saving Service emerged as a separate entity and Sumner Kimball became its General Superintendent, an office which he held with distinction for many years. It will be seen that all these major improvements in the sea rescue organisation took place during the relatively long period of peace which the USA enjoyed after the Civil War. Indeed, it is remarkable that the young nation was able to achieve so much in what was possibly not considered a matter of high priority at the time. This in spite of the fact that USA shipyards had shown the world how to build the fastest of clipper ships and the country was the nearest rival to Britain in shipping tonnage in 1870. But sail was rapidly giving way to steam although it was not until 1885 that the 'kettles' could claim to have exceeded the total tonnage of the 'windbags'.

In the early part of the twentieth century, the Life Saving Service controlled 13 districts – 9 on the Atlantic coast, 3 on the Great Lakes and 1 on the Pacific coast. There were 210 rescue stations on the Atlantic coast, 61 on the lakes and 19 on the Pacific coast making 281 in all. It is interesting to note that this compares almost exactly with the number of lifeboat stations in Britain at the same time.

In the USA, the stations were divided into three classes: Life saving, Lifeboat and House of Refuge. The life saving stations were normally two storey buildings, the lower portion housing the lifeboat and the upper the life saving or line-throwing gear. The Lyle wreck gun was one of the line-throwers, firing a 17 lb projectile and reputed to have a range of 700 yards. As with the projectile of Captain Manby's mortar, it must have been a fearsome thing as it hurtled towards a stranded vessel. No doubt it was considered to be a calculated risk!

In charge of each station was the Keeper, who in 1912 was

paid $1000 (then about £200) a year. The boat's crew, known as surfmen, were paid $65 (then about £13) a month for their annual period of service and $3 a day if required at other times. Volunteer helpers were also rewarded. It will be seen that the wages bill came to a fairly considerable sum for those days.

The early lifeboats and their crews

The boats mainly used were a form of surfboat known as the Beebe–McLellan self-bailer, which was about 25 ft long with a beam of 5 ft, carrying a crew of seven. This type of boat weighed about half a ton and launched off a special carriage, the crew running her out through the surf and tumbling aboard as she floated off. The boat was freed of water taken on board by means of relieving tubes through the bottom, which cleared her quickly. Capsizes were frequent and with this and the method of launching the crew must have been in the water nearly as much as they were out of it. As most of their work was in winter it can have been no picnic. There can be little doubt that they were fine, hardy seamen and apparently strong swimmers. In this latter they differed considerably from their opposite numbers in British lifeboats with whom swimming was an unusual accomplishment in those days. There are a great number of stories stressing the heroism of the men who manned the life saving surfboats of the early rescue service and of their devotion to duty, which cost many of them their lives.

Although in the hands of hardy, capable seamen these surfboats were able to survive extreme conditions they must have appeared flimsy cockleshells to the distressed mariners they were used to rescue. Many of the lives lost from surfboats were entirely due to the crews being hampered by frightened survivors, who tended to panic, perhaps not unnaturally, rather than help their rescuers. The reason for the light build and general characteristics of the surfboat was, of course, the necessity for launching the craft off an open beach in bad weather by the crew alone, since a heavier type of boat would have made launching impossible. Even today, with fairly sophisticated launching carriages, tractors and other aids, getting a boat afloat off an exposed beach in onshore gales is a hazardous operation needing great skill and judgement. In the USA, lifeboats are no longer launched over beaches.

Not only were the surfboats used for the rescue of shipwrecked mariners, but also on more than one occasion they were used to evacuate people from the shore when hurricanes in the Gulf of Mexico destroyed rescue stations and devastated stretches of coastline. Boats put to sea with women and children on board and remained afloat through what must have been a long night of terror, exposed to the wild fury of the storm.

The surfboats which over such a long period formed the main rescue fleet of the USA were in fact a unique American development. During the 1870's and 1880's, the most popular surfboats were the local types based on either the Sea Bright skiff of New Jersey or the whale boats and saine boats

Surf boat of the Orleans Lifesaving Station near Cape Cod, Mass. coming ashore in 1908. The men are wearing the old-style cork lifejackets – but 1908 was also the year when kapok was being recommended for use in lifebelts in the USA.

used in New England fisheries. As in other countries, the men preferred the craft they were used to, and it no doubt took a long time to persuade them that there could be anything better. The Race Point and Monomoy surfboats may have evolved from the whale boat and saine boat and were the favourite types on the New England coast.

After the formation of the US Life Saving Service the lifeboat which evolved was clearly a descendant of the RNLI self-righter and this connection continued right through to the 1950's when the development of the present day '44 footer' instituted a radical change in American lifeboat design.

The possibilities of the internal combustion engine were quickly appreciated in the USA and it is possible that there was less scepticism on the part of the crews of rescue craft there than amongst the British lifeboatmen. Many surfboats were fitted with 8 hp gasoline engines; on the Great Lakes a larger boat, similar to the British self-righter was favoured and these had 30 hp engines installed in the after end-box, giving a speed of 7 knots or more.

Formation of the Coast Guard Service

In 1915 the Revenue Cutter Service and the Life Saving Service were amalgamated to form a new organisation to be known as the Coast Guard, headed by a Captain Commandant. The original ten vessels requested by Alexander Hamilton had grown into a great fleet with many duties, covering an enormous length of coastline. It was laid down that in wartime the new service should become an integral part of the US Navy, but in peacetime should operate as an independent force under the control of the Treasury. This meant that the Coast Guard had a bare two years to become accustomed to its new guise before it was called upon to exercise its warlike role as a part of the navy in World War I. In 1967 the Coast Guard became part of the new Department of Transportation.

The loss of the *Titanic* with 1,517 of her passengers and

crew after she struck an iceberg led to the formation of an International Ice Patrol. This was decided at a conference of the principal maritime nations in London in 1914 and they agreed to share the cost in suitable proportions. The duties were in fact taken over by the Revenue Cutter Service which had already started ice patrols. In due course the newly formed Coast Guard assumed the responsibility and, except for breaks in wartime when the patrols were suspended, they have continued this lonely and difficult duty every since. Aircraft are now used almost entirely for this work.

Between the World Wars the Coast Guard organisation grew considerably. To some extent this was due to the duties which devolved upon it for the enforcement of prohibition. Dealing with the rum-runners was a difficult and at times highly dangerous business. Also, it was not generally popular so it can hardly have been a happy time for the Coast Guard crews who nevertheless carried out their duties in an exemplary fashion.

Throughout the war the Coast Guard service maintained and indeed increased its gallant reputation and it would be easy to go on relating interesting and successful exploits. But it will be appreciated that in a book devoted to sea rescue, the wartime achievements of the Coast Guard cannot be included other than where these involve life saving or may be considered to have some relevant interest. In fact, it is only possible to sketch brief details of sea rescue incidents and the many exciting stories of actual rescues have already filled several books and will no doubt fill many more.

The Coast Guard command was quick to appreciate the value of aircraft for rescue work, particularly for locating casualties whose position was not known accurately. With their comparatively slow speed and limited range of vision, surface craft are unable to search large areas quickly and thoroughly. In good visibility an aircraft with trained observers can cover large stretches of ocean in a fraction of the time a ship would take. So, by 1916 the Coast Guard was already operating its own air section and although this was no doubt brought into being by wartime requirements, it remained to do invaluable service in peacetime and to become a major factor in modern sea rescue techniques.

The ability of the helicopter to hover and lift or scoop up survivors without having to alight brought new possibilities of quick rescue into everyday practice. The Coast Guard set up a special helicopter training base in 1943 and in the first year passed out 150 mechanics and 100 pilots as fully qualified. Some of the most daring and effective rescues have been carried out by helicopter, such as that of the crew of a crashed Royal Canadian Air Force plane who were found and brought out from the icy shores of Goose Bay in Labrador in 1945 and eighteen survivors from a Belgian air liner which crashed in wild country near Gander in Newfoundland. When the National Search and Rescue plan was adopted in 1956 this reaffirmed the responsibility of the Coast Guard for the co-ordination of rescue operations in the maritime regions. Today, the aviation division of the Coast Guard operates fourteen different types of aircraft including helicopters and gigantic flying boats. The largest flying boats have a radius of action of 1,500 miles and use a special jet-assisted take-off.

The USCG today

Today, with a fleet of splendid cutters of up to 3,000 tons, another great fleet of lifeboats for inshore work and the impressive aviation division, it must be conceded that the US Coast Guard controls a vast and efficient organisation. But this only covers a portion of the assistance rendered to seamen by the Coast Guard. In addition, all lighthouses, lightships and other coastal navigational aids such as buoys and beacons are also the responsibility of the Coast Guard and although not strictly a matter of sea rescue are certainly a means of preventing disaster. In all, over 44,000 navigational aids are maintained, in itself a monumental task. The tenders which service the 25,000 buoys marking dangers and channels carry out many other valuable duties, performing

Flood victims of hurricane 'Agnes' in 1972 being rescued in Harrisburgh, Pa. by US Coast Guard Boating Safety detachments.

rescue work of all sorts while some also work as ice-breakers when necessary.

In the Great Lakes, at one time closed to navigation by ice from fall until well into spring, the Coast Guard ice-breakers now keep channels open much later in the year and break new channels so that movement can commence much earlier in the year.

Three weather ships or ocean station vessels in the Atlantic and one in the Pacific are operated by the Coast Guard. These ships cruise in small, carefully defined areas reporting weather conditions and assisting ships and aircraft to avoid dangerous storm centres. Weather ships on their station have carried out dramatic rescues, the cutter *Bibb* taking off 69 survivors from a flying boat which ran out of fuel and came down alongside her in waves 35 ft high. Apart from their valuable reports the weather ships, battling it out with the fearsome western ocean 'greybeard' waves, provide a comforting rescue facility for aircraft and small vessels crossing the long stretch of angry ocean, with fine, calm spells few and far between, even in summer.

US Coast Guard 44 ft (13.4 m) steel lifeboat rescues a survivor from a capsized boat. In 1974 the Coast Guard answered 20,000 calls for assistance and saved 42,000 lives.

Wartime experience and the development of new materials and techniques have naturally been reflected in the design and construction of new lifeboats for the Coast Guard. The major development has been that of the 44 ft lifeboat which evolved as the result of exhaustive investigations and trials. Powered by two diesel engines each producing 180 shaft horsepower and of welded steel construction, this type was built to replace the famous 36 ft motor lifeboat which had done yeoman service over so many years and whose design had not changed significantly since the first self-righter was imported from Britain. This fact is of particular interest since the reverse process took place in 1964 when the RNLI purchased a 44 ft lifeboat from America and subsequently built a small fleet to a slightly modified design.

Utility boats and ships' lifeboats have also undergone development investigations and trials, during which many years of coxswain and crew experience was used to obtain data and assist evaluation. As a result a Coast Guard design

Winter patrol – a US Coast Guard 52 ft (15.8 m) lifeboat in heavy surf at Yaquina Bay, Oregon. These routine patrols operate in the roughest coastal waters of the USA.

was adopted and twenty-four boats in aluminium alloy are in production at the Coast Guard yard.

Nowadays, the search and rescue resources of the US Coast Guard are varied and extensive, as may be seen from the table:

US Coast Guard fleet

Facility	Dimensions	Number
Boats		
Patrol boats	95 ft (29 m)	26
Patrol boats	82 ft (25 m)	53
Motor lifeboats	52 ft (15.8 m)	4
Motor lifeboats	44 ft (13.4 m)	92
Motor lifeboats	36 ft (11 m)	26
Utility boats	40 ft (12.2 m)	140
Utility boats	30 ft (9.1 m)	130
Launches	17 ft (5.2 m)	80
Aircraft		
Twin-engine amphibians		36
Amphibious helicopters		105
Lifeboat stations		153

The US Coast Guard cutter *Chase* heading for the open sea from her homeport of Boston, Mass. She is 378 ft in length and was built in 1968 in New Orleans. She is also the third cutter in the USCG's history to be named after Salmon P. Chase, Secretary of the Treasury under President Abraham Lincoln. The 80 ft flight deck, which can be seen towards the stern of the vessel, can accommodate the USCG's latest rescue helicopters.

In addition, the Coast Guard fleet includes a large number of sea-going cutters and vessels of various types normally engaged in other duties but which may be used for rescue work if necessary.

Gallantry

It is not easy to choose an example from the many gallant sea rescues carried out by the Coast Guard force but the following account describes briefly one of the most complex and dangerous missions ever undertaken. It is perhaps of special importance from the seaman's point of view in that no helicopters took part. No doubt the airman will consider that the whole operation would have been very much easier had they been able to do so.

Over the weekend of 16–17 february 1952, a winter storm raging off the coasts of Massachusetts and Maine was

The bow portion of the tanker *Pendleton* off North Beach, Mass. No survivors were found here but thirty-two men were rescued from the after part. The vessel broke in two during hurricane force winds in 1952.

increasing in intensity. Coast Guard cutters and a flying boat had searched unsuccessfully for a missing New Bedford fishing schooner which was later known to have been lost with all hands. Off Cape Cod at 06.00 on Monday 18 February in hurricane force north-east winds, a high sea and blizzard conditions, the 10,000 ton tanker *Pendleton*, bound for Boston, cracked a welded seam and tore apart into two helpless sections; 8 of her crew were left on the bow portion and 33 on the after part. The disaster happened so suddenly that it was impossible for them to send out an SOS and the plight of the ship was not known to anyone else for eight ghastly hours.

Survivors being rescued from the after part of the tanker *Fort Mercer* which broke in two on the same day as the *Pendleton* and not far away from her. In all, seventy men were rescued from the two tankers by the US Coast Guard.

Some 30 miles away and about 23 miles east of the Pollock Rip Lightvessel, another tanker of the same type, the *Fort Mercer*, was battling with similar storm conditions. She was bound for Portland, Maine, from Louisiana with a full cargo of fuel oil. Just before 08.00 a seam in her number five starboard tank fractured and the process of disintegration began. Her captain decided that it would be impossible to turn the ship and run for shelter in the existing conditions so he contacted the Coast Guard by radio telephone and asked for an escort to his destination. Meanwhile, every effort was made to nurse the damaged ship through the mountainous seas although it was clear that she was taking enormous punishment and losing buoyancy forward. At noon on 18 February, there was a rending, grinding scream of tortured metal as the bow section parted agonisingly from the stern portion which carried the engines and some of the accommodation. The captain was on the bridge, which was on the bow section, and there were 8 men with him. There were 34 men on the stern portion and they had barely had time to take in the extent of the catastrophe when the bow, driven by a fierce squall, took a sudden sheer and bore down on them. The engines were still working in the stern portion and the Chief Engineer gave the order for full speed astern and narrowly averted what may well have been a fatal collision.

The first vessel to join the *Fort Mercer* was a cargo ship in ballast, the *Short Splice*, and she herself was finding it all she could do to weather the storm, but she immediately offered to stand by until conditions allowed her to make an effort at rescue.

Thus began the long and arduous rescue operations in which eventually four Coast Guard cutters, three lifeboats and a tug took part together with over a thousand officers and men. A Coast Guard seaplane also took off and located the stern portion of the *Fort Mercer*. A radar station at Cape Cod picked up two unidentified objects which proved to be both parts of the *Pendleton*. The seaplane pilot was able to confirm that there was not one casualty but two, and in four pieces!

The Chatham lifeboat crossed the bar in terrifying conditions and fought her way to the stern portion of the *Pendleton*, which at first appeared to be deserted but later the coxswain, Bernard Webber, with great skill and courage, rescued 32 men and got them safely ashore. The Stage harbour lifeboat found the bow portion which originally sheltered 8 men but here there were no survivors.

The two portions of the *Fort Mercer* were drifting farther and farther apart. The wind was north-east, 55 knots, with heavy breaking seas. The cutter *Yakutat* rescued the

Injured survivors from the bow portion of the *Fort Mercer* being taken aboard the US Coast Guard cutter *Yakutat*.

survivors from the bow portion using rafts and also a whale boat with Ensign Kiely in charge. Four men who jumped for the rafts did not reach them and drowned.

Meanwhile, 45 miles to the northward, the stern portion of the *Fort Mercer* was riding out the storm on an even keel. Nearly twenty-four hours had passed since the accident when the cutter *Eastwind* arrived, followed shortly by the Coast Guard tug *Acushnet*. By clever manoeuvring Lieut. Commander Joseph of the *Acushnet* placed the stern of his vessel alongside the casualty and in two attempts 18 men were taken off. At this point 13 men decided to remain on board and did so until the stern portion was towed to safety. Of the crews of the two tankers 14 died and 70 were saved. Of the rescuers, 21 were decorated for gallantry.

Canada

The Canadian Shipping Act requires all Canadian vessels to go to the assistance of any vessel in distress, providing that they can do so without endangering themselves but the Department of Transport prefers to use government ships where possible in order to minimise disruption of commercial activity. In 1952 the Department of National Defence was authorised to establish rescue co-ordination centres for the control of rescue operations with Coast Guard rescue officers attached to the RCC's to advise and assist with marine rescue work. In addition the Department of National Defence has established composite rescue squadrons of Labrador helicopters and Buffalo aircraft and the Coast Guard has deployed a fleet of cutters and small craft as primary rescue units.

The Canadian Coast Guard today

The first line of defence against marine casualties is therefore the Coast Guard rescue units and the Canadian forces rescue squadrons, all of which are on call at all times. Next come other Coast Guard ships and aircraft together with ships and aircraft of other government departments. In addition all commercial and pleasure craft and aircraft are expected to render any assistance within their power should the occasion arise; and finally there are several hundred volunteer rescue agents who assist with communications and rescue operations generally.

On Canada's east coast the CG ships *Alert* (234 ft, 71.3 m) and *Daring* (178 ft, 54.2 m) are based on Dartmouth, Nova Scotia and patrol the outer fishing banks. The CG ship *Rally* (95 ft, 30 m) is also based on Dartmouth and patrols the coastal fisheries and the Gulf of St Lawrence. Three 44 ft (13.4 m) steel lifeboats of the US type are based on Clark's harbour, Westport and Fisherman's harbour, Nova Scotia. Four more boats of this type are being built for the Newfoundland coast.

The cutter *Relay* patrols the St Lawrence river and a 40 ft

Canadian Coast Guard 40 ft (12.2 m) steel lifeboat *Mallard* stationed at Vancouver, BC. Speed 18 knots.

(12.2 m) launch is based on Quebec. Three 67 ft (20.4 m) cutters patrol Lake Ontario, Lake Erie and Georgian bay and a 40 ft launch is based on Trenton, Ontario with a 32 ft (9.7 m) launch at Amherstburg.

On Canada's west coast, three 95 ft (30 m) cutters are based on Victoria, British Columbia and 44 ft lifeboats are stationed at Banfield, Tofino and Bull harbour. Two 40 ft launches are based on Vancouver and an SK45 Hovercraft at Vancouver airport. A larger hovercraft, an SRN6 built in the U.K. at Cowes, Isle of Wight, has also been acquired.

Inflatable rescue boats similar to the ILBs of the RNLI are being tested on the west coast. The boats are crewed by students and each unit is in the charge of a regular Coast Guard officer. The students are employed for the summer months and receive training in small craft operation and rescue techniques. Initial results have been favourable and it is likely that the system will be extended.

Crews of all Coast Guard and service craft are employed full time and the rescue services dealt with 2,168 incidents in 1971. Both fixed wing aircraft and helicopters are used for rescue work, principally for searching, leaving marine craft to complete the task, although helicopters are used to take people off vessels.

It is interesting to note that the Canadian Coast Guard not only report increasing work for the rescue services from the ever growing number of people taking their recreation afloat, but also what appears to be a general decline in self-reliance on the part of seafarers of all types. It would seem that more and more people afloat expect the state to look after them, rather than look after themselves. This is indeed a change of attitude from that of the seamen of old, who were nothing if not self-reliant and who tended to look on any operations of the government of the day as bearing more relation to a clenched fist than a helping hand! But there is still some individual enterprise and on the Great Lakes there are private rescue organisations, often supported by local authorities, with rescue stations and boats manned by vol-

Canadian Coast Guard 69 ft (21 m) rescue cutter *Spindrift*.

unteers. These organisations work in conjunction with the Rescue Co-ordination Centres and constitute a valuable link in the marine rescue system of the country.

At the time of writing the Canadian Coast Guard search and rescue fleet was made up as shown in the table:

Canadian Coast Guard fleet

Type of boat	Number
Offshore patrol cutters	7
Great Lakes patrol cutters	3
Shore-based launches	5 (+ 1 reserve)
Shore-based lifeboats	10
Shore-based hovercraft	1

Hovercraft

The Canadian Coast Guard first considered the possibilities of air cushion vehicles in 1965 and chartered a Bell SK5 (which was a modified British Hovercraft Corporation SRN5) for trials on Lake Ontario in 1966. As a result, an SRN5 was purchased from Britain and modified for search and rescue. It was stationed at Vancouver because the

Canadian Coast Guard SK5 Hovercraft based at Vancouver Airport.

Georgia Strait between Vancouver island and the mainland was likely to produce suitable weather conditions for operational trials. Also, the large number of floating logs encountered in the strait gave the hovercraft distinct advantages over surface craft.

The SRN5 arrived from Britain in June 1968 and training of crews started immediately. Full operation started in April

1969 and in the two years to the end of March 1971 the craft logged 2,000 hours operating time during which 245 search and rescue missions were carried out.

The craft proved to be very seaworthy and can operate in the Georgia Strait in winter gales of up to 50 knots and seas of 8 ft in height, although it is said that these conditions are difficult for the crew. This seems more than likely. A maximum speed of 55–60 knots is possible in fine weather. Speed drops off rapidly with rising seas, but even at the limit of its seakeeping capability, the hovercraft can maintain a higher average speed than a surface craft of similar size.

Searching ability is restricted owing to the low height of eye and the blind area astern, but this is to some extent offset by the greater area covered in a given time. Towing is practicable but somewhat awkward, although a number of successful towing operations have been carried out, including one involving a 56 ft (17 m) fishing vessel.

The hovercraft has proved particularly effective for shallow water work, ice conditions and for reaching places inaccessible by other means, as may be appreciated from the following account.

In December 1968, before the hovercraft rescue station at Vancouver was considered fully operational, a request was received for assistance to a 70 ft (21.3 m) vessel on the rocks of Stuart island, some forty miles away. Conditions were severe with high wind and seas, poor visibility and pan ice. A helicopter had taken off one person but had had to abandon further efforts owing to the high wind and nearby cliffs.

On leaving her base at the international airport the hovercraft crossed 10 miles of pan ice and then ran into very rough water. At the small cove where the casualty was aground, the wind speed was 35 knots driving sheets of water up to ten feet above the surface of the sea. The hovercraft was taken stern first into the cove, passing over rocks projecting 2–3 ft out of the water. Seas were bursting over the stranded vessel and the rescue craft and her crew.

In spite of these appalling conditions, the rescue was

carried out successfully and the survivors transferred to a US Coast Guard cutter which was standing by in the lee of a small island. The operation involved a total distance of 80 nautical miles and 50 minutes were spent at the scene of the accident. The total elapsed time was 3 hours 10 minutes.

To end the description of sea rescue hovercraft on what might be considered a somewhat facetious note – but which emphasises the extent of human fallibility – it is necessary to give an account of the one occasion on which the Vancouver hovercraft was seriously damaged. This happened during a search along the shore on a warm summer night. The searchlight was switched on suddenly and fully illuminated a girl about to enter the water, delightfully nude. At this moment the craft commander reported that he experienced a sudden 'rudder overbalance' and the hovercraft hit a concrete post!

The Caribbean Sea and the Atlantic

Bahamas

One of the latest additions to the organisations in touch with the International Lifeboat Conference is the Bahamas Air–Sea Rescue Association which maintains 4 lifeboats and has the services of a number of auxiliary rescue craft. Of these, 3 lifeboats are stationed at Nassau and 1 at Freeport.

Bermuda and Curaçao

Other sea rescue organisations of which details have recently been received are the Citizen's Rescue Organisation of Curaçao, in the Netherlands Antilles, and the Bermuda Search and Rescue Institute based on Hamilton, Bermuda in the Atlantic. The Bermuda Institute operates a 30 ft (9.1 m) offshore rescue boat and a 15 ft (4.6 m) inshore rescue boat. Both these craft are jet-propelled as the wide area of coral reefs in which they operate precludes the use of propellers.

The 30 ft (9.15 m) jet rescue craft of the Bermuda Search and Rescue Institute. Provided primarily as an air crash rescue boat, she is also used for offshore sea rescue and is designed to work over coral reefs.

CHAPTER FOUR

EUROPEAN ORGANISATIONS (1)

The Netherlands

The Netherlands has two lifeboat institutions and both were formed in November 1824, within a few days of one another. The first, the North and South Holland Lifeboat Institution (NZHRM), undertook to provide rescue arrangements on the Dutch coast north of Scheveningen and the other, the South Holland Institution for Saving the Shipwrecked (ZHRM) agreed to be responsible for the remainder of the Dutch coastline to the southward. The reason for this decision was the influence of the Netherlands pilotage authority, which took an active interest in the formation of the rescue organisations and who similarly divided the coastline as convenient for administration.

The immediate cause of the demand for better sea rescue

Dutch KZHRM lifeboat *Koningen Juliana*, of the Hook of Holland station, in heavy seas.

Dutch KNZHRM lifeboat *Carlot* of Terschelling on service. Wreck of the Greek ship *Panagathos* in the background.

facilities was the loss of the Dutch frigate *De Vreede* off Den Helder in 1824, with heavy loss of life. Some sturdy fishermen put off in a small boat and succeeded in saving some lives, but a second attempt ended in tragedy as the boat capsized and all but one rescuer were lost. There was a national outcry at the loss of life in this disaster and some public-spirited citizens immediately called for support to provide proper sea rescue arrangements on the Dutch coast. In fact, there had been boats stationed on the coast for rescue purposes for many years but as with other countries, without a proper organisation they did not prove satisfactory. During the reign of Louis Napoleon as King of Holland, six boats of the Greathead design were built in the country and stationed at key positions on the coast and it would seem that a state run lifeboat service was envisaged. Probably in view of the political situation this did not become fully established and the loss of the *De Vreede* emphasised the need for a proper rescue service. The meetings held in Amsterdam and, a few

145

days later, in Rotterdam were successful in obtaining public support and the two sister organisations commenced their long and valuable career.

The earliest Dutch lifeboats were built of wood and many were of the Norway yawl type, propelled by oars. Sailing cutters were in use about the middle of the nineteenth cen-

Rescue of the crew of the Greek vessel *Panagathos* by the KNZHRM lifeboat *Carlot* and helicopters.

Launch by tractor of the Dutch KNZHRM lifeboat *Kurt Carlsen* of Noordwijk.

tury and were also built of wood originally but later steel was used. In 1864, the ZHRM obtained some lifeboats from Britain, built to the RNLI design and in 1893 purchased a steam-driven, water jet-propelled lifeboat to the design of R. & H. Green and named *President van Heel*. This lifeboat was stationed at the Hook of Holland and went to the assistance of the British railway ferry steamer *Berlin* in 1907, when she was lost with nearly all her passengers and crew on the pier at the entrance to the river Maas. The *President van Heel* capsized in 1921 with the loss of all her crew of six, but was salved and continued in service until 1930, two years longer than the last British steam lifeboat. In 1909, a sister boat *Prins der Nederlanden* was built in Holland and did very well until she, too, capsized in 1929 with the loss of her crew of eight. Between 1873 and 1891 a number of self-righting pulling and sailing lifeboats were built in Holland of mahogany and one of these was fitted with a 27 hp petrol engine in 1907. She was destroyed by a petrol explosion in 1920. The first motor lifeboat built as such was the *M. C. Blankenheym* which was launched in 1912 and fitted with a 76

147

hp paraffin engine. She was 56 ft in length with a beam of 16 ft and had a speed of 8 knots. It will be noted that this was a very large boat, compared with any RNLI lifeboat of that period and this tendency continued, not only in the Netherlands but in other European countries apart from Britain. The RNLI did build some 60 ft boats between the wars and two 70 ft rescue cruisers in 1964 and 1965.

Today, the ZHRM maintains 8 rescue stations using motor lifeboats, inflatable boats and rocket apparatus. Of these, the Hook of Holland is the major station with a 70 ft (21.3 m) boat driven by two 200 hp diesel engines giving a speed of 11 knots and also a 33 ft (10 m) boat capable of 8 knots. It is possible that a second station on the south bank of the river will be established in view of the Europort developments there. Since 1824, the South Holland rescue service has saved over 4,600 lives in a total of 728 successful sorties.

Rescue of the crew of Chinese ship *Wan C...* by Dutch lifeboat usin... breeches buoy n... Ijmuiden.

The KZHRM fleet in 1975 was composed of three rescue cruisers 69 ft (21 m) long and one of 58 ft (17.8 m). Also three lifeboats 32 ft (9.8 m) one of which was launched by carriage and tractor. There were three inshore lifeboats of the RNLI Atlantic type, 21 ft (6.45 m) in length.

The two Dutch lifeboat services work in close collaboration and even have a combined letterhead on which to communicate jointly. Both are, and have always been, entirely voluntary organisations although their fund raising activities differ to some extent. The South Holland organisation (ZHRM) obtains the bulk of its revenue from 'ship contributions', a small sum added to accounts by shipping agents dealing with vessels visiting the major Dutch ports, under the heading of 'lifeboat contribution'. Since the number of ships calling at Rotterdam is very much more than at Amsterdam the South Holland organisation is able to raise the bulk of the money required in this way. On the other hand, the North and South Lifeboat Institution has a

Still launched by horses – the KNZHRM lifeboat stationed at the Isle of Ameland.

much bigger list of subscribers and the necessary income is mainly due to this source. To some extent the division of the coastline into two parts with separate administration of the rescue services was influenced by the channelling of local revenue and support. There have been two state commissions of inquiry into the efficiency of these voluntary life saving organisations in Holland and in each case there was a unanimous decision that the government should not interfere with their working. Both organisations were granted the prefix 'Royal' by Queen Wilhelmina in 1949 on the occasion of their 125th anniversary, so that their correct initials are now KNZHRM and KZHRM. These stand, respectively, for *Koninklijke Noord-en-Zuid-Hollandsche Redding-Maatschappij* and *Koninklijke Zuid-Hollandsche Maatschappij tot Redding van Schipbreukelingen*. It is not necessary to give either organisation its full title when asking for assistance!

Throughout practically the whole of their existence the Dutch rescue organisations have worked in close contact with the RNLI and from this co-operation some lasting friendships have resulted. Many problems have been common to both countries and with seamen in particular there are no frontiers to humanitarian efforts. It is not possible within the space available to give a substantial history of Dutch sea rescue but there are a number of details which demand inclusion.

In the early days of this century the NZHRM maintained 32 rescue stations of which 2 had rocket installations only. The fleet consisted of some 30 boats in all; 22 of them being 'surf' or 'strand' boats, 2 were self-righters, 2 motor lifeboats and the remainder 'vlets', a flat-bottomed type with a pronounced sheer used in shallow, sheltered waters. The surfboats were specially suited to working off flat, sandy beaches as they were light and easily transported and launched. They were nearly 28 ft long by 8 ft beam, fitted with air cases and 8 relieving tubes which cleared them of water very quickly. It is interesting to compare these boats and their use with those used by the rescue service in the

An unusual rescue device used by the Dutch KZHRM and known as a 'walking net' (*left*). The net used to remove an injured man from a vessel (*right*).

United States. The self-righters were similar to those of the RNLI and were 34 ft long with a beam of 8 ft. Again there is an interesting comparison between the length to breadth ratios of the surfboats and self-righters. The self-righters were both pulling and sailing boats.

One motor lifeboat was stationed at Scheveningen. This boat, the *Jhr J. W. H. Rutgers van Rozenburg* was built in 1907. She was 38 ft long and fitted with a 45 hp Brooke engine. The other, the *Brandaris*, was stationed at Terschelling. Built in 1910 she was over 57 ft long and fitted with a 76 hp Kromhout engine giving her a speed of $8\frac{3}{4}$ knots. This fine vessel, certainly one of the most able lifeboats in her time, was lost with her crew of four on service in 1921. An account of this disaster is given in Chapter eight. After both world wars great changes in lifeboat design followed technical advances. After the first International Lifeboat Conference in 1924, there was close contact between many of the rescue organisations, which helped to make full use of the technical information available.

Today, the NZHRM controls 25 rescue stations along the North Sea coast and in the Ijsselmeer. The fleet consists of 11 motor lifeboats of which 6 are self-righters, 13 beach motor lifeboats and 4 flat-bottomed motor launches. The motor lifeboats are stationed in the North Sea harbours and along the coast of the Ijsselmeer; the other boats are used for inshore rescue work and over mudflats and sandbanks. At the Hollum station in Ameland, 10 horses are still used to pull the boat and carriage into the water. Fourteen of the stations are equipped with line-throwing apparatus. Since 1824 the NZHRM has saved over 10,500 lives.

As with Britain, the Dutch lifeboatmen are mostly volunteers, but full-time men are employed in boats which require constant maintenance. The volunteers come from all sorts of occupations as seamen and fishermen are not necessarily on hand when a lifeboat is called out. But the available crews, whether building or factory workers, shopkeepers, mechanics or any other trade, all have a seafaring background and know their coastal waters intimately.

Norway

Norway's rugged coastline extends some 1,400 miles, of which almost half lies within the Arctic Circle. Great fjords reach into the mountainous interior and myriads of islands fringe the steep shores. In the early days sea transport must have been the only practical way to carry goods and people any distance and bad weather could hardly have failed to take its toll. Indeed, in the middle of the nineteenth century, the sea claimed over 700 lives annually out of a population of barely $1\frac{1}{2}$ million.

In 1854 a number of rescue stations were established on the south coast of Norway on the lines of those existing in Great Britain, but for a number of reasons a shore-based service did not provide an adequate answer to the sea rescue

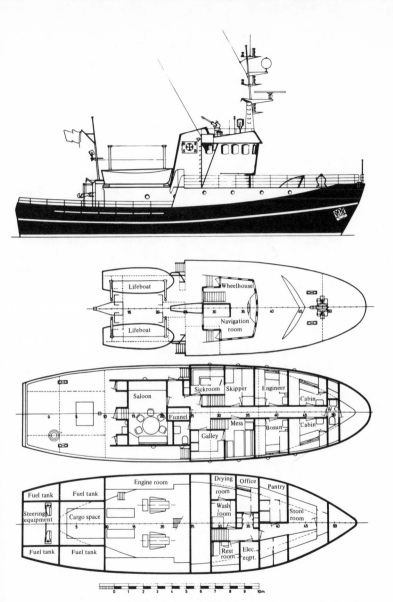

Profile and deck plan of the Norwegian rescue cruiser *Ada Waage*. She has a length of 80 ft (24.4 m), an operating speed of 20 knots and was built in 1975.

problems. It was not until 1891 that positive steps were taken to overcome the difficulties and it was then largely due to the efforts of one man, Dr Oscar Tybring. As a result of his exertions, the *Norsk Selskab til Skibbrudnes Redning* (NSSR), the Norwegian Society for the Rescue of the Shipwrecked, was established with the help of the Merchants' Society of Christiania.

Because of the great length of coastline, which would have needed many lifeboat stations to provide adequate protection, and because of the movements of the fishing fleets, it was decided that rescue vessels must be able to remain at sea and patrol where required. A well-known naval architect, Colin Archer, designed and built a 42 ft rescue ketch to be handled by a crew of four and able to remain at sea for considerable periods in any weather. This vessel proved highly satisfactory and she was named *Colin Archer* after her designer. In 1893 she rescued 36 people off the coast of Finnmark in a hurricane. This incident created widespread interest and enthusiasm, many supporting societies being formed to raise funds for additional boats. As a result, by the end of the century there were 13 life saving ketches regularly on patrol at sea, and by 1907 there were 20. The Colin Archer type of vessel, a ketch rigged double ender, gained popularity all over the world and many may still be seen afloat today. This applies to the original *Colin Archer* which was given to the Maritime Museum in Oslo after being taken out of service. She has been used as a training craft for sea schools.

Until 1930, the Norwegian rescue craft were all sailing vessels and so well were they built and handled that in spite of being afloat continuously in all weathers and during the long arctic winter, only three were lost. In 1930, the first engine was installed in one of the ketches and between 1935 and 1940 fourteen motor vessels with auxiliary sails were commissioned. These new vessels were 62 ft in length and fitted with radio telephones and echo sounders. Undoubtedly, they were well-equipped, seaworthy vessels and were able to stand comparison with any other lifeboats in use at that time.

During World War II, no new lifeboats were launched, but the fleet was kept intact in spite of many difficulties. At the end of 1945 many replacements were needed, as with most other European rescue organisations. Norwegian fisheries extended to distant waters, from the Shetland islands, Hebrides and the west of Ireland to Iceland and the coasts of Greenland. In order to assist the fishing fleets at such distances, it was necessary to build larger rescue craft of which the first was a new type of cutter built in 1949. Since 1958, 27 new steel cutters have been built; 6 of 55 ft (16.8 m) for coastal work, 3 of 87 ft (26.5 m) for ocean and coastal service, 13 of 75 ft (22.9 m) for general service and a 92 ft (28 m) vessel for long distance work. In addition, two lifeboats of the US Coast Guard 44 ft (13.4 m) steel type have been built for inshore work. Two 80 ft (24.4 m) rescue cutters, developed from the popular 75 ft (22.9 m) type and the powerful 92 ft ocean-going vessel, were under construction for delivery in 1973–74. All these rescue vessels are gifts from private persons or firms connected with shipping.

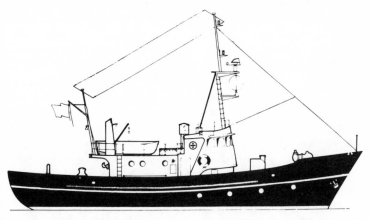

Profile of the Norwegian rescue cruiser *Jørgen Amudsen*. Length 74 ft (22.6 m).

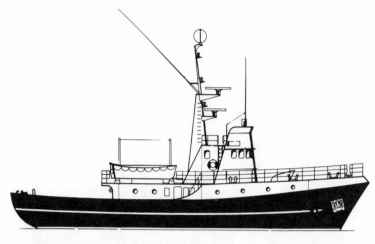

Profile of the rescue cruiser *Sjøfareren*. She is 93 ft (28.4 m) long and has a service speed of 12 knots.

Originally the wooden ketches only operated during the five months October to April, but this has gradually been extended and today rescue craft are on duty for ten months of the year. During the summer season, four cutters are kept in service, one at the North Cape, one near Aålesund, one at Egersund and one at Lerwick in the Shetland Islands. This last, as the Norwegians politely put it, 'With your permission'. During the winter months there are 32 rescue craft stationed at various points between Halden and Kirkenes keeping a twenty-four hour watch on the distress frequency. Two main rescue co-ordinational centres are located at Bodø airport and the Sola airport at Stavanger and there are six local centres. Since 1970, the Department of Justice has been responsible for all rescue service in Norway and the local rescue centres operate under the chief of police of the district. This is not entirely popular with the NSSR but the society continues to do its job as efficiently as ever. All sections work in close conjunction with the Royal Norwegian Navy and Air Force and with harbour authorities. The Norwegian government has recently purchased 10 Westland 'Sea King' helicopters for rescue work. Many British seamen have had reason to be thankful for the efficiency of the Norwegian rescue service. In the winter of 1951 the rescue ketch *Larvik* saved the crew of 24 of the British ship *Solidarity*, 50 miles off the coast of Romsdal in a full gale and heavy sea. This is but one incident and in all since 1891 the Norwegian rescue fleet has saved 4,550 people of different nations and assisted some 60,000 vessels, a record of which even the sea-hardy Norwegians must be proud.

The Norwegian rescue service today has an imposing fleet consisting in the main of rescue cruisers ranging from 55 ft (16.75m) overall to 93 ft (28.36m). The older vessels were built of wood but the later craft are of steel. The smaller craft of the lifeboat type have aluminium hulls. About 60 % of the NSSR running costs comes from state funds.

Sweden

In spite of apparent similarities between the coastline of Sweden and that of Norway the rescue problems of the two countries differ considerably. Much of the Baltic coast is icebound in winter and the Swedish lifeboats have to deal with many calls for assistance from among the thousands of islands that lie offshore. The southern and western coasts border busy shipping lanes and elsewhere the increasing popularity of water sports, always favourite recreations in Sweden, have kept the rescue services busy.

Although the need for organised sea rescue was first suggested in 1810 the proposal was not implemented although local boats were no doubt used when possible. In 1852 the Royal Naval Club at Carlskrona became interested in the development of sea rescue in Denmark and articles were published calling for the establishment of rescue stations at a number of key points. Again, no progress appears to have been made as a result.

In 1854 the Swedish parliament decided to establish a lifeboat service and two rescue stations were opened in southern Sweden and equipped with lifeboats and line-throwing apparatus. For the first sixteen years the service was controlled by the Royal Swedish Navy, but in 1870 it was transferred to the Pilotage Board and by 1900 the number of rescue stations had increased to fifteen.

Disasters in 1903 and 1904, when many ships were wrecked on the west coast with great loss of life, were widely reported in the press and led to criticism of the adequacy of the rescue facilities. As a result of efforts of the Swedish Shipping Society, a large sum of money was obtained from public donations and the Swedish Sea Rescue Institution, *Svenska Sallskapet for Raddning af Skeppsbrutne* (SSRS), was formed in June 1907. It was modelled on the lines of the RNLI in Britain, a compliment also paid by a number of other countries.

Swedish rescue helicopter and rescue cruiser *Dan Broström*. Stationed at Käringön, she is 78 ft (23.8 m) long and has a speed of 12 knots.

Swedish inflatable rescue craft stationed at Mariestad. Length 15 ft (4.65 m) and speed 30 knots.

In 1912, the rescue service completed its first three motor lifeboats and in 1917 built a rescue cruiser for patrol work. Sweden shared the necessity for this latter type of vessel with Norway, whose experience with them possibly influenced the decision. Both countries had large fleets of fishing craft, often working considerable distances from their home ports and the rescue cruisers were able to move around with them, providing on the spot protection which shore-based lifeboats could never achieve.

In 1955, a government committee was set up and charged with the duty of investigating the organisation and efficiency of the sea rescue services in Sweden. The conclusion reached was that the existing system was a fine example of co-operation between a government service and a voluntary institution. Some small changes were made and the result was the sea rescue system which obtains today. It was laid down that as far as possible use should be made of all available craft and manpower for rescue purposes. This included pilot cutters, customs' craft, naval vessels and air force planes. The Sea Rescue Institution supplements these facilities and provides special lifeboats with voluntary or full-time crews. All co-operate as necessary under the co-operation of the coastal radio stations.

Today, Swedish lifeboats are built of steel and are generally about 40 ft (12.2 m) in length with a single screw working in a tunnel and a speed of 9 knots. The rescue cruisers are up to 75 ft (22.9 m) in length with speeds of over 12 knots.

The Swedish rescue craft frequently have to operate in severe ice conditions, sometimes acting as ice-breakers for the fishing fleets. In January 1962 a rescue cruiser was asked to try and return 17 people from the mainland to their homes on the island of Holmo, which they could not reach because of the ice. In the pitch darkness of a January night, with increasing wind and drifting pack ice, the cruiser herself became trapped. Eventually, the skipper managed to man-oeuvre his ship clear but could not get nearer than 700 yards from the island. The hardy islanders disembarked on to the rough, hummocky ice and made their way towards the shore of the island, watched by the crew of the rescue cruiser. Hardly had the party reached the shore when the ice broke up and drifted rapidly seawards. Under the pressure of the ice the rescue cruiser nearly rolled over but recovered and set course for her base.

In spite of all the hazards with which they have to contend the Swedish rescue cruisers and lifeboats have an enviable reputation for safety. Throughout the whole existence of the service no rescue craft have been lost and only three lifeboatmen have lost their lives.

By 1972, the SSRS fleet consisted of 10 rescue cruisers of about 70 ft (21.3 m), 10 steel lifeboats of about 40 ft (12.2 m), 3 high-speed aluminium lifeboats capable of 20 knots and 3 inshore inflatable boats similar to those used by the RNLI.

Finland

To the student of sea rescue organisation, that of Finland may well prove one of the most interesting and worthy of careful study. There are certainly strong indications of lively and practical minds responsible for the management of this institution which has had to weather some very stormy periods during its existence.

The Finnish Lifeboat Society (*Suomen Meripelastusseura*) was founded in Helsinki in March 1897, its charter giving it the task of rescuing distressed mariners in the coastal waters and lakes of Finland. The first rescue station was established on the island of Lavansaari, followed by one at Valassaaret near Vaasa. An important event was the building of the Society's first motor lifeboat, which was completed in 1913 and stationed at Hankö at the entrance to the Gulf of Finland. The first lifeboats were manned entirely by lighthouse keepers, pilots and fishermen but this no longer applies. As in many other countries, crews today are drawn from all walks of life and all sorts of trades and professions.

World War I halted progress for the time being but afterwards the now independent Finland re-opened rescue stations and ensured that boats and equipment were in serviceable condition. Conditions were not easy and funds were eroded by inflation so that some stations had to be closed and no new equipment could be provided.

After World War II a complete new programme was planned and by 1963 the fleet consisted of 12 motor lifeboats and 4 rescue cruisers with 14 shore stations equipped with line-throwing apparatus. Much of Finland is icebound in winter and the rescue craft have to be of steel construction to stand the pressure of ice, and indeed to act at times as ice-breakers.

Today the Society maintains 30 lifeboat stations with volunteer crews numbering about 300. Six of the rescue vessels are of the cruiser type between 57 ft (17.4 m) and 67 ft (20.4 m) long. Sixteen lifeboats are of wood or glass-reinforced plastic construction and between 37 ft and 43 ft (11.3–13.1 m) long. A 43 ft steel lifeboat has been built and five of the existing craft are built of steel and used for ice-breaking. All vessels have a speed of about 10 knots.

The Society operates through 33 branches which include ladies' committees whose task is to raise funds. The necessary finance comes from some 7,000 subscribers and other voluntary means, aided by funds from some state controlled agencies.

On the Finnish lakes, the Society helps the police authorities who, as they say, 'are more or less landlubbers' and organises boat owners to assist them. They also co-operate with flying clubs who carry out search duties over the archipelago and close contact is maintained with the Red Cross, many of whose volunteers man the lifeboats. If helicopter assistance is required, this is requested from the Finnish Air Force by the Coast Guard. In general, the organisation may be taken as an excellent example of making the best use of everything and everybody.

There is a separate organisation in the Åland islands which operates a $55\frac{1}{2}$ ft (16.9 m) lifeboat and an inflatable.

Denmark

A quick glance at the map of Denmark is enough to convey the necessity for an efficient sea rescue service in that country, which has a very extensive coast line for its size. The flat, sandy west coast of Jutland is exposed to the full force of the North Sea gales from south-west to north-west and it has been the scene of many disastrous wrecks. One of the worst incidents occurred in 1811 when two British ships of the line drove ashore and were smashed to pieces in a fierce gale. Of the combined crews of 1,400 men, only 17 were saved.

The first effort to provide means of rescue for shipwrecked mariners was made by a man named Hansen of Svaneke who provided a lifeboat for the island of Bornholm. Little more appears to have been done until 1845 when Christopher Berend Claudi put forward a proposal for the establishment of a Danish life saving service and submitted it to the Customs Authority and Chamber of Commerce. He made tremendous efforts to interest people in sea rescue and eventually persuaded the Danish Shipping Society and others to

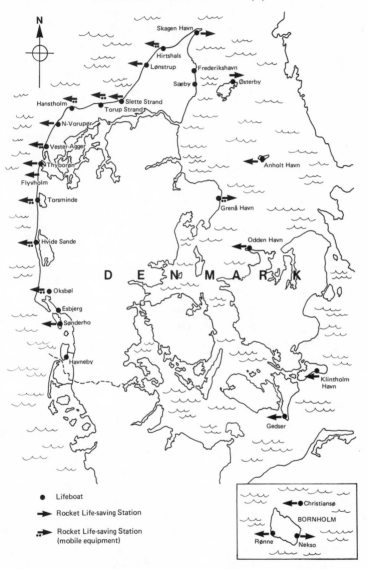

Type and location of sea rescue facilities for Denmark.

raise funds for lifeboats. As a result two boats were provided and stationed at Flyvholm and Klitmoller in 1846. Two sets of rocket apparatus were bought from Britain also.

Claudi had taken a lively interest in life saving at sea for many years and had studied the working of the RNLI in Britain with some care. He had also had some first-hand experience of sea rescue and in 1847 he was present at the wreck of the barque *Vertumnus* at Harboore beach. On this occasion he made several attempts to rescue members of the crew, unfortunately without success, and there is no doubt that the tragedy made a lasting impression on him.

The Danish government took an interest in the efforts made by Claudi and eventually sent him to Britain to make a further study of the organisation there. On his return he became a member of a commission which put forward a plan for a state life saving service. This was approved and in March 1852 legislation was passed which brought the Danish Rescue Service, *Redningsvaesenet*, into being.

In 1976 the service was reported to have 25 motor lifeboats in service. Recently a well-known firm of naval architects in Copenhagen has designed a new type of self-righting lifeboat about 50 ft in length with a speed of about 10 knots. This is the first Danish built self-righter and it is understood that others of the same class are now in service.

Iceland

The National Lifesaving Association of Iceland, *Slysavarnafjelag Islands*, was founded in January 1928 and its first lifeboat came from the RNLI. This was the *George and Mary Berrey*, a 35 ft self-righter which had been stationed at Whitehills in Scotland from 1901 to 1928. She was renamed *Porsteinn* and stationed at Sandgeroi. Today 126 life saving and rocket stations are maintained round the coast of Iceland. The rescue service maintains 3 lifeboats and 1 inshore lifeboat. More rescue craft are planned. In conjunction with private owners and pilots the association operates hospital and search aircraft which have proved of great value. The association has some 200 branches throughout Iceland and about one person in six of the population is a member.

A great deal of attention is paid to educational work in the prevention of accidents. This aspect is considered of equal importance with the actual rescue work as Iceland has a high personal accident rate both at sea and ashore. During forty-three years of rescue work, well over 6,000 people have been saved at sea off Iceland and well over 2,000 vessels assisted. In spite of differences of opinion over fishing in the waters round Iceland, British and other trawlermen have good reason to be grateful for the Icelandic rescue services and many fishermen owe their lives to the skill and bravery of the Icelanders.

CHAPTER FIVE

EUROPEAN ORGANIZATIONS (2)

West Germany

The sea rescue organisation in Germany began with the establishment of life saving stations on the Baltic coast by the government of Prussia. This was shortly after the great exhibition in London in 1851 when the Duke of Northumberland's lifeboat design competition had aroused world-wide interest in the subject. It was not until 1860, when the brig *Alliance* was lost near Borkum with all hands, that further efforts were made to extend the rescue service. As a result of this disaster, two gentlemen of Vegesack near Bremen, an instructor of navigation named Bermpohl and a lawyer named Kuhlmay, appealed for the foundation of a German national organisation on the lines of the RNLI. In fact, a number of local societies were formed and that of Emden established lifeboat stations on the islands of Borkum, Juist, Norderney, Baltrum, Langeoog and Spiekeroog, and on the mainland at Neuharlingersiel and Carolinensiel. In addition, a Manby mortar was placed on Juist.

In 1865, another attempt was made to establish a national organisation to co-ordinate the efforts of the different societies already established and those projected. In March of that year a meeting took place at Kiel which resulted in The German Society for the Rescue of the Shipwrecked *Deutsche Gesellschaft zur Rettung Schiffbrüchiger* (DGzRS) being formed with headquarters in Bremen. This successful outcome was largely due to the untiring efforts of Dr Emminghaus of that city. New stations were opened and at the turn of the century there were over 120 in operation.

The lifeboats used were principally of the British 'Peake' design or the American patent 'Francis' type. The 'Francis' was built of sheet iron and was double-ended with end-boxes, but no self-bailing devices. The latter went through several stages of modification to become what was known as the 'German' lifeboat. In due course, practically all German lifeboats were built of steel and in the early 1900's were said to cost about £125 and a boat carriage £75.

As was the case with the RNLI in Britain, the national organisation in Germany gradually absorbed the local societies and by 1885 had taken over control of the Prussian State stations in the Baltic. From the outset the lifeboat service was supported entirely by voluntary contributions but inflation after World War I put the organisation into difficulties and it had to appeal to the state for help. This was given in the shape of small subsidies but the situation did not last for long and the rescue service was soon back to working on an entirely voluntary basis.

Considerable technical progress was made between the wars and many boats were fitted with engines and radio sets. The capabilities of the motor lifeboats made it possible to reduce the number of stations and at the outbreak of World War II the German rescue organisation consisted of 101 rescue stations with 84 lifeboats and 68 rocket installations. After the end of the war in 1945 the activities of the DGzRS were confined to West Germany – the Federal Republic – which had 23 rescue stations. Funds were nearly exhausted and once again state aid had to be accepted in order to maintain the essential service. But by 1957 the organisation had become soundly based again and the state subsidy was relinquished as the voluntary system was considered to be by far the best for lifeboat work. The difficulties of a voluntary rescue organisation in the light of political and domestic upheavals such as Germany has experienced twice in a short lifetime can hardly be exaggerated. That the Society has survived and surmounted the stupendous obstacles is a measure of the stability of this great service.

Since 1945 very considerable advances have been made in the design of boats and equipment and the rescue stations have saved many lives. Over 13,000 people have been rescued off the German coast since records began, and of this number, a very large proportion have been saved in the last twenty years. The German North Sea coastline is flat and sandy, broken by sandbanks and islands with wide areas of shallow water between them and the mainland. Here, there are innumerable channels and small craft are frequently in trouble. As the new, larger motor lifeboats were introduced, it was clear that their necessarily increased draught was going to limit them to the channels on many occasions and for work in the very shallow water, small, flat-bottomed lifeboats were stationed at key points. It was decided that all boats should be designed with great initial stability and that self-righting ability should be incorporated. In very shallow

One of the newest German rescue cruisers, the *John T. Essberger*. She was delivered to the DGzRS in May 1975. Length 146 ft (44.5 m) and a range of 600 miles at 30 knots, or 2,000 miles at 15 knots.

water, self-righting moments could be seriously impaired.

For some cases, neither the large motor lifeboat nor the shallow draught boat was entirely suitable. The first because of her deep draught and the other because of lack of power and sea-keeping ability. A very great deal of thought was given to this problem and the result was the powerful rescue cruiser with a speed of over twenty knots. Housed on a slipway in a recess in her stern she carries a 'daughter boat' some 20 ft in length and capable of being launched in any weather. The 'daughter boat' is recovered by the reverse process, being manoeuvred into the stern opening of the parent vessel, from which position she is winched up the slipway to her stowage place.

These large rescue cruisers proved highly satisfactory, a number of others being developed from the prototype with modifications suggested by operating experience. Eventually seven rescue cruisers were completed and stationed at key points close to the main shipping routes, namely Borkum, Heligoland, Amrun and at the mouths of the Weser and Elbe rivers. Two others are stationed in the Baltic near Kiel.

It then became necessary to replace a number of beach boats owing to age and in deciding on the most suitable design for the new craft consideration was given to the changing pattern of casualties. Just as round the coasts of Britain, the upsurge of yachting and boating activities was being felt by the German rescue service and this was a major factor in the decision to build a much faster type of craft. This was based on the large rescue cruiser design and also equipped with a daughter boat. With an overall length of 55 ft (16.8 m) and a beam of $12\frac{1}{2}$ ft (3.6 m) the accepted design had a draught of $3\frac{1}{2}$ ft (1 m) and a speed of 17 to 19 knots. All welded light alloy construction with a special lattice framework was chosen in order to ensure that the beach boat can withstand heavy grounding and impact with casualties. Her small daughter boat is just under 15 ft (4.6 m) long with a beam of $5\frac{1}{2}$ ft (1.7 m) and draws $1\frac{1}{2}$ ft (0.5 m), being powered by a standard inboard motor.

Helicopter about to touch down on the *John T. Essberger* during the boat's early trials.

German navy rescue helicopter lifts a survivor from the deck of the *John T. Essberger.*

DGzRS statistics for 1971 make impressive reading with reports of 993 operations carried out and 1,361 people rescued. Of 473 major casualties 249 were yachts or pleasure craft and 126 fishing vessels.

At the 21 stations maintained by the organisation there were 25 rescue craft made up as shown in the table:

West German lifeboat fleet

Type	Number	Operating speed (knots)
Rescue cruisers with daughter boats	8	19–24
Smaller rescue craft with daughter boats	4	18
Beach lifeboats	12	8–12
Others	5	

A new rescue cruiser, 146 ft (44.5 m) overall with a beam of 26½ ft (8.05 m), of light alloy construction and capable of a speed of 30 knots went into service with the DGzRS in the latter half of 1975. Named *John T. Essberger* the new cruiser is fitted with a comprehensive outfit of navigational and communication equipment, a hydraulic crane and sophisticated fire-fighting appliances. A helicopter platform is fitted aft over the daughter-boat stowage and although primarily designed for hovering pick-up and delivery has proved very satisfactory for actual landing, even in rough weather.

This is undoubtedly one of the most advanced rescue craft designs extant and extensive trials have proved the vessel capable of a wide range of duties.

East Germany

The sea rescue service of the German Democratic Republic,

East German type R17 rescue cruiser *Arkona*, built in 1974.

East German lifeboat *Poel* built in 1954. Length 59 ft (17.9 m), speed 10 knots.

Seefahrtsamt der Deutschen Demokratischen Republik, operates nine rescue stations. Two of these have rescue cruisers and two are equipped with lifeboats. Four stations have mobile rocket gear and inflatable rescue craft and the remaining station rocket equipment only.

The 2 lifeboats were built in 1954 and details are as follows:

Length overall	58½ ft (17.97 m)
Breadth	17 ft (5.15 m)
Draft	6½ ft (1.97 m)
Speed	10 knots

Belgium

The Belgian sea rescue organisation was established by the state in 1838 and since the coastline is only some 35 miles in length the requirements were not extensive. In the early part of this century there were 8 rescue stations of which the major ones were at Nieuport, Ostend, Blankenberge and Heyst. The others were at Adinkerke, Coq, Zeebrugge and Knocke. The coast is generally sandy and flat and the boats were mostly of shallow draught, drawing less than 1 ft of water and they were about 30 ft long. They were fitted with air cases and selfbailing devices, but were not self-righters. They were transported on iron carriages, which were pulled by teams of horses if required to launch at some distance from a station. A larger lifeboat was stationed at Ostend and she was towed to the scene of the wreck by one of the state-owned tugs of the port. Motors had been installed in the lifeboats at Zeebrugge and Blankenberge by the year 1910. Crews were paid a retainer and there were also volunteers who agreed to man the boats if required. Both the permanent crews and the volunteers received rewards for going to sea on service.

As with other nations involved in World War II, Belgium suffered losses of boats and equipment. Three 46 ft (14 m) Watson type lifeboats as used by the RNLI were built at Cowes by J. Samuel White and stationed at Ostend, Zeebrugge and Nieuport. Each of these stations also has a rocket life saving apparatus mounted on a lorry equipped with radio telephony.

In addition there are two state-owned tugs at Ostend, one of which is always in readiness. The rescue organisation works in close collaboration with the Belgian Navy, Air Force and Red Cross.

At the end of 1976 the sea rescue service was reported to be undergoing reorganisation and the Watson type lifeboats built at Cowes in 1948 are to be replaced. A RNLI Arun type lifeboat is under construction for Belgium.

France

In 1865 the Emperor Napoleon III ordered the establishment of a sea rescue service to be known as the *Société Centrale de Sauvetage des Naufragés*. There were a number of lifeboats and rescue stations round the coast of France and the object of the new organisation was to increase their efficiency by bringing them under one control. The RNLI, established some forty years earlier was used as a model and boats were built on similar lines to those used in Britain.

The crews were mostly recruited from local fishermen and

A French pulling lifeboat of 1892 with carriage and horses. She was stationed at Cayeux on the river Somme.

longshoremen and they received payment for their services when called out, in a similar manner to that obtaining in Britain.

Internal combustion engines were fitted in lifeboats experimentally from 1912 but World War I interrupted progress and it was not until 1918 that real headway was made with power-driven lifeboats. From then on, the use of power-driven boats became general and the last sailing lifeboat was put into service in 1923. The advantages of diesel engines for lifeboat work were quickly appreciated, in view of their reduced fuel consumption and smaller fire risk. In 1939, the society had 6 lifeboats driven by twin diesel engines of between 24 hp and 40 hp. By that time the total fleet consisted of 105 lifeboats of which 44 were engined. This compares with the RNLI fleet of 165 in 1939 of which 145 were power driven.

The Society suffered great damage and losses of boats during World War II and in 1945 virtually had to make a fresh start. Fifty-six lifeboats equipped with diesel engines were projected, and although at the time this was considered to be enough to give ample coverage, the upsurge of boating and sailing and indeed of all water sports made it necessary to provide fast inshore rescue facilities at many resorts.

In 1873, eight years after the founding of the Central Society, Nadaud de Buffon founded the Breton Humane Society whose first purpose was to assist the families of lifeboatmen who lost their lives on service. Later, its activities were extended to helping shipwrecked people generally and eventually to equipping rescue stations on the coast of Brittany and on its rivers. The society received official recognition as a public service in 1895 and it would appear to have well merited this distinction if only for the astonishing scope of its activities. These included the award of a first prize for the unsinkable boat *Henry* at the World Exhibition and the launching of the first motor lifeboat in 1904; the creation of the first fishing schools and the

Fast offshore rescue craft *Anne de Bretagne* of the French SNSM, stationed at le Croisic (Loire-Atlantique).

provision of fishing vessels with a small hospital unit on board, also insurance for fishermen and the promotion of safety regulations. In many ways the society sought to improve the lot of fishermen and ensure the safety of seafarers generally. Major congresses were held on the subject of safety at sea and many foreign nations sent representatives, leading to many new developments. In 1905 the Breton Society maintained 16 rescue stations on the coast, several lifeboats, 200 river stations and various arrangements concerned with safety on shore. Dr Patay, medical inspector of the society, was a leading exponent of resuscitation of the apparently drowned. The society was one of the first organisations to concentrate on the safety of bathers and others using beaches, providing resuscitation apparatus and first-aid posts at 300 different stations.

As with the Central Society, World War II saw the destruction of nearly all the Breton Society's equipment and after the war their new president, M. Lepeltier, set about re-establishing the stations. This mammoth task continued until 1958 when Paul Renault took over and carried on the work. At this time the necessity for secondary life saving stations became apparent owing to the tremendous increase in yachting, boating and other water sports, as had been experienced in other countries.

The Breton Society was one of the first organisations to appreciate the possibilities of inflatable craft driven by powerful outboard engines and soon had some 90 stations equipped with Zodiac-type inflatable boats. The ease with which these inflatables can be launched, their high speed and low cost make them ideal for beach rescue work and many countries have adopted them.

In May 1967, the Minister for the Merchant Marine decided that it would be in the interests of efficiency and economy for the two life saving societies to merge and that a single organisation should be responsible for all sea rescue work off the coasts of France. Under the title of *Société Nationale de Sauvetage en Mer* (SNSM) the new organisation

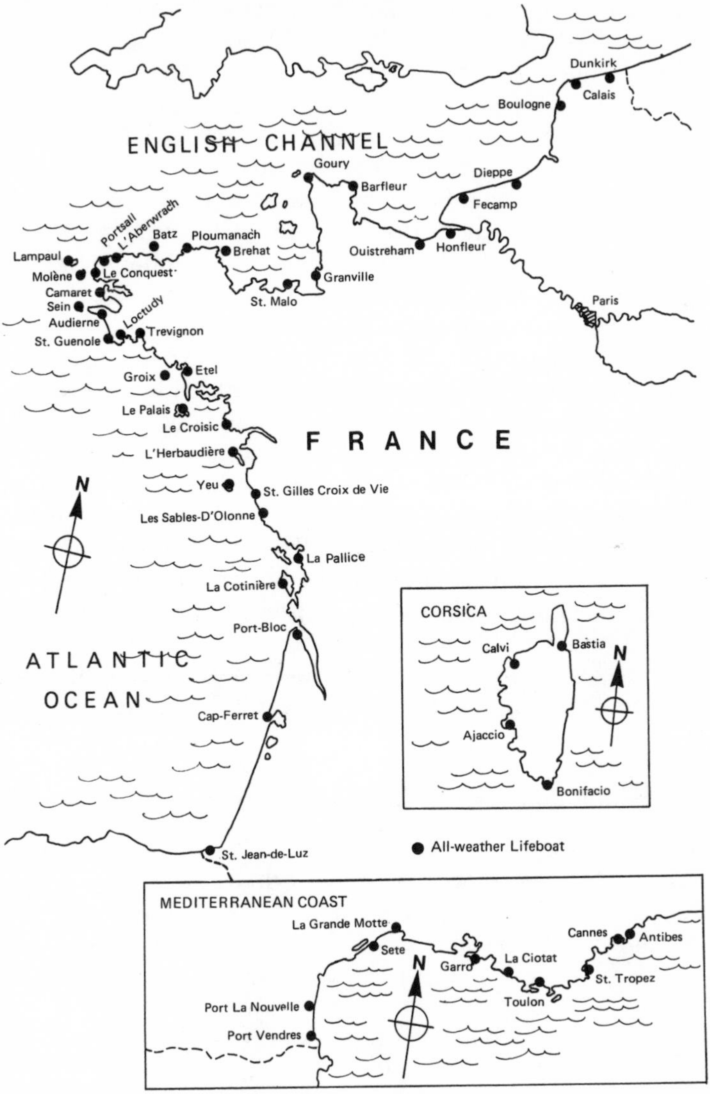

Location of SNSM stations in France.

came into being on 1 January 1968 under Admiral Amman as President and with Vice-Admiral d'Harcourt as President d'Honneur.

By 1971, the fleet consisted of 5 conventional lifeboats, 93 inshore rescue boats of modified commercial design, 268 inflatable boats and a variety of auxiliary, training and ancillary craft. There are 271 rescue stations of which 157 operate all the year round and 114 in summer only. The budget for 1970 was about $5\frac{1}{2}$ million francs and in that year 579 lives were saved and 2,253 craft assisted.

The rescue craft are manned by volunteer crews with some additional assistance from the French Navy and the Gendarmerie during the busy summer months. Finance is provided as to approximately one-third by the government, one-third by local authorities and one-third by voluntary contributions.

An interesting new French lifeboat, *Commandant Gaudin*, was completed in 1971 by Franco-Belge Shipbuilders at their yard at Gennevilliers, near Paris. She is 50 ft (15.2 m) in length with a speed of 14 knots, is fitted to take four stretcher cases and has fire fighting equipment.

The SNSM now maintains no less than 274 lifeboat stations (7 in the West Indies) and the fleet consists of:

    52 'All-weather lifeboats'

    90 fast vedettes

    286 inflatable inshore lifeboats.

Switzerland

It may come as a surprise to learn that not only is there a flourishing rescue organisation in Switzerland, the *Société Internationale de Sauvetage du Leman*, but also that it is reported to operate no less than 74 lifeboats. These are stationed at various strategic points on the Swiss lakes and have no doubt proved their worth in the sudden storms which can arise on these extensive areas of water.

Spain

The Spanish Society for Life Saving at Sea (*Sociedad Española*

Spanish all-weather rescue craft of the Nivel 'A' category, for work off the Atlantic coast. Length 51 ft (15.5 m), speed 14 knots.

de Salvamento de Naufragos) was founded in 1880 largely owing to the efforts of Martin Ferreiro who was employed in the Spanish Hydrographic Office. He had been compiling statistics of shipwrecks on the coast of Spain and was alarmed to find that some 1,800 people had lost their lives in this way over a period of fifteen years. He launched a campaign in the press appealing for the formation of a sea rescue service and promptly received the support of the royal family. He was also helped by Admiral Rubalcava who became the first president of the society.

In January 1887, the society received official recognition by the government and assumed responsibility for such services as had been provided by the state in the past. It became

Spanish inshore rescue craft of the Nivel 'B' type, for use in the Mediterranean. Length 20½ ft (6.3 m), speed 25 knots.

Fleet of Spanish inflatable rescue craft of the Nivel 'C' type; speed 25 knots.

responsible for the maintenance of existing lifeboats and received an annual grant for this purpose. From this time on the essential work of life saving on the coasts of Spain was carried out effectively until the period of the civil war, 1936–39. During this time the society suffered many losses and although replacements were made, economic and other difficulties did not allow it to recover its earlier standards.

On 22 February 1971 the Conde de Toreno became president of the society when a complete reorganisation of its facilities was planned. In addition, a new society known as the Spanish Red Cross of the Sea, *Cruz Roja del Mar*, and associated with the Spanish Red Cross was formed and amalgamated with the original society. In the autumn of 1971, two RNLI lifeboats visited Spain at the request of the *Cruz Roja del Mar*. Both boats were new and of new types which the Spanish society wished to evaluate. One was a $48\frac{1}{2}$ ft (14.8 m) Solent class boat presented to the RNLI as the result of a highly successful appeal by the Royal British Legion and the other was a 52 ft (15.8 m) prototype of the Arun class which was undergoing extensive trials.

While carrying out trials off the Spanish coast the Solent class boat, the *Royal British Legion Jubilee* went to the assistance of a Spanish trawler aground in fog and picked up her crew from their life raft. She then towed the trawler off safely. On her return to Britain, the *Royal British Legion Jubilee* was named by Her Majesty the Queen at a special ceremony.

At present, the Spanish rescue fleet consists of 5 rescue cruisers, 13 lifeboats and 247 inshore lifeboats. All rescue activities are undertaken in conjunction with the search and rescue organisation of the Spanish Navy, Air Force, Red Cross and Salvage organisation.

Type and location of sea rescue stations in Spain.

Portugal

In 1879, a committee was appointed to examine the organisation of life saving services in Portugal under the chairmanship of Admiral Jose Baptista de Andrade. In the course of its deliberations the committee studied details of similar organisations abroad including those of the Life Saving Institution of Marseilles and the RNLI. It also collected statistics of wrecks in Portugal, Madeira and the Azores with a view to deciding on the places where lifeboats and rescue equipment were most necessary. Since it was clear that the extensive requirements could not all be met at once, an order

Naming ceremony launch of the Portuguese lifeboat *Commandante Couceiro* in 1962.

of priority was made, based on the incidence of shipwrecks over a nine-year period. The report also contained suggestions as to the type of lifeboats considered suitable and for the provision of medical and other assistance for shipwrecked people.

On this basis, the *Instituto de Soccoros a Náufragos* was formed in 1882 with Queen Amelia of Orleans and Braganza, wife of King Carlos I, as president. There had been various local rescue stations prior to this time and, as in many other countries, the need for co-ordination and national support had become increasingly necessary. One thing at least was not lacking, and that was brave and experienced seamen to man the boats, since every mile of Portugal's coastline could provide lifeboatmen as required.

When Portugal became a republic, the Institution had 31 pulling and sailing lifeboats, 23 sets of line-throwing apparatus and other equipment at various stations round the coast.

Throughout the two world wars and up to the present day, the Portuguese rescue service has continued to work and improve its organisation and equipment. Two lifeboats built in 1962 were named after outstanding personalities of the service. The *Commandante Couceiro* was named after a former director and chief inspector of the Institution, who died in 1961, and the other *Patrao Rabumba* after a coxswain of the Leixoes lifeboat who had carried out many gallant rescues and who had received many decorations, both Portuguese and foreign.

The necessary finance is raised by voluntary contributions with state subsidies. Crews are mostly volunteers with full-time men employed where necessary.

At the time of writing there were 21 lifeboats and 65 inflatables of the inshore type in operation. In addition, 24 'Land-Rover' vehicles with trailers carrying line-throwing and other equipment are used for rescue from shore. Rescue work is carried out in co-operation with the Customs, Police and Fire Brigades with assistance from the Army and Navy as necessary. One of the latest additions to the fleet is a lifeboat to the 37 ft Oakley design of the RNLI, built in Portugal. In 1977, two RNLI Waveney and two RNLI Oakley lifeboats were under constuction.

Italy

The Italian Society for Rescuing the Shipwrecked, *Societa Italiana di Soccorso di Naufraghi*, was founded in 1871 and was very active in the days of sailing ships when there were numerous wrecks on the coast of Italy. With the coming of steam the number and type of casualties changed considerably and the activities of the society diminished. It was found impossible to maintain shore rescue stations along the whole 5,000 miles of coastline and funds were used to reward people carrying out rescues in their own boats. But in 1932 the society decided to build a motor lifeboat and also to organise rescue work by using vessels which attended on fishing fleets to carry the catches to the shore. All craft employed were fitted with radio sets so that they could receive immediate information about casualties.

Today the Navigation Code and Maritime Law place the responsibility for sea rescue on the Ministry of Merchant Marine. The effective organisation is headed by the Inspector General of Port Authorities. The rescue services of the port authority, the *Capitanerie di Porto*, are based on two systems; the use of the port authority craft manned by service personnel and the employment of any other vessels and craft as available and suitable. The port authority craft consist of the three main classes set out below and based on possible weather conditions and the type of rescue work envisaged.

Maritime police and fast rescue services
For this work high-speed motor boats are used and they are not normally expected to operate in more than moderate sea conditions.

Rescue services under severe conditions
Various types of lifeboats and rescue craft of other nations

Italian 85 ft (26 m) rescue cruiser *Michele Fiorillo,* of the German design, about to launch the 'daughter-boat'. The CP 212 fast rescue launch stands by.

have been evaluated for this work and a number are now in service and others being built. Five 52 ft (15.8 m) lifeboats of the RNLI Barnett type were built by Groves and Gutteridge Ltd of Cowes and are stationed at Bari, Civitavecchia, Cagliari, Trapani and Carloforte. Fast rescue cruisers of the German *Georg Breusing* and *Theodore Heuss* type have been built and 2 lifeboats of the USCG 44 ft (13.4 m) steel type are stationed at Ancona and Pescara. In all, some 200 lifeboats are maintained.

Italian rescue craft of the 40 ft (12.2 m) Keith Nelson type. Speed 21 knots.

Inshore rescue and first aid

For this work fast inflatables of types similar to the RNLI inshore lifeboats are used together with GRP craft of the dory type. An interesting innovation is the provision of inflatable rescue platforms accommodating 120 to 150 people. These are carried by some of the rescue craft and might well be of great value in the event of a major aircraft or ferry disaster.

Coast Guard service in the vicinity of ports is undertaken by sea-going launches of from 35–40 ft (11 m to 12 m) long.

There were 2,209 rescue operations carried out in the five years 1966–70, with 1,569 people saved and assistance rendered to 640 vessels.

The Italian Navy and Air Force assist with major rescue operations as necessary.

Turkey

The country has a lengthy coastline of varying aspects, extending from the border with Syria in the most easterly part of the Mediterranean, then round in a big arc through the Aegean to the Dardanelles; thence through the Sea of Marmara, the Bosporus and along the whole of the southern shore of the Black Sea to the border with the USSR. Much of this coastline is subject to violent northerly winds and smaller vessels in particular are quite frequently in danger.

The Turkish sea rescue service is controlled by the state owned Turkish Maritime Bank, which provides the necessary finance. Facilities appear to be concentrated in the Black Sea and divided into three districts for administrative purposes. These are Rumeli on the European side, and Anadolu and Kefken on the Anatolian side. Five lifeboats are maintained and there are twelve stations equipped with rocket apparatus. Five successful rescues were carried out in 1971.

In 1950, a 35½ ft (10.8 m) lifeboat of an RNLI design was completed by Groves and Gutteridge of Cowes, Isle of Wight, for the Turkish rescue service. It was powered by a Perkins diesel engine.

CHAPTER SIX

THE SOUTHERN HEMISPHERE

Argentina

The search and sea rescue organisation is under the control of the Commander in Chief of the Navy, the executive responsibility being shared by the Argentine Naval Prefecture and the Naval Operations Command.

The rescue stations are as follows:

Argentine Naval Prefecture
  Buenos Aires
  Mar del Plata
  Bahía Blanca
Naval Operations Command search and rescue centres
  Buenos Aires
  Mar del Plata
  Puerto Belgrano
  Ushuaia

The Naval Prefecture maintains vessels for patrol, sea rescue, coastguard and fire fighting. The Naval Operations Command operates vessels of the 'Reglain' class and 'ATA' class and also lifeboats. Crews are employed full-time, or are serving naval personnel who carry out rescue work in addition to their other duties. Aircraft of the Short Skyvan type are used for coast patrol work. In 1970, forty-four emergencies were dealt with by the rescue services off the Argentine coast.

The Naval Operations Command only intervenes in rescue work when it is considered that the Naval Prefecture has exhausted its resources.

Brazil

The sea rescue service of Brazil is known as the *Servico de Busca e Salvamento da Marinha* (short title, *Salvamar*) and is

Brazilian naval rescue tug *Tridente*.

under the supervision and co-ordination of the naval operations command.

The service maintains 5 rescue stations and operates 13 rescue vessels. These vessels consist of tugs and corvettes of

Corvette *Forte de Coimbra* of the Brazilian Navy, used for sea rescue work.

the *Tridente* and *Forte de Coimbra* classes. Both fixed-wing aircraft and helicopters are used to supplement surface craft in rescue operations and all crews are employed full-time.

In 1972 the rescue service dealt with 96 casualties.

Chile

The Valparaiso Life-boat Volunteer Institution, *Cuerpo de Voluntarios de los Botes Salvavidas de Valparaiso*, was founded in 1925 by Captain Oluf Christiansen as a means of safeguarding the lives of ship's crews during the heavy north to north-west gales that endanger vessels in the Bay of Valparaiso during the winter months. From 1925 until 1957, the rescue work was carried out by a former RNLI lifeboat built in 1905, and a smaller boat built by the Thornycroft company in 1920. In 1955, the Institution bought an ex-RNLI

The Valparaiso, Chile, lifeboat. She is a Watson type lifeboat, purchased from the RNLI.

lifeboat of the 46 ft (14 m) Watson type and fitted her with two Gardner 4 LW engines. No hull overhaul was necessary and only a small amount of re-wiring, in spite of the fact that this boat was built in 1925.

The Valparaiso Institution is a private, voluntary organisation, financed by voluntary contributions and a small government grant. The membership is drawn from all walks of life in the country and does not boast one professional seaman in its ranks. As the organisers put it, 'All our experience has been gained the hard way in the Bay of Valparaiso during winter storms'. This may be taken as an excellent example of the essential spirit of lifeboatmen.

Whenever the wind is in the north and of more than force 4, the lifeboats provide the only link between ships at anchor and the shore. Their work includes landing sick passengers or crew, assisting vessels tied up to buoys to reinforce their moorings, taking crews marooned on shore off to their ships.

One pleasant incident reported was a call from a Chilean naval vessel riding out a storm in the bay. The message asked if an officer could be landed as he was due to be married in a couple of hours' time. The duty was gladly carried out but it was rather cynically noted in the record that it was not known whether the officer in question was subsequently grateful or otherwise!

Recently the Institution has extended its activities and has assisted in the formation of other rescue organisations in the country at Talcahuano and Coquimbo. It is pointed out that there is no other organisation able to render rescue service in Chile of the type carried out by the Valparaiso Institution.

Uruguay

The *Asociación Honoraria de Salvementos Maritimos y Fluviales* (ADES) translates its name into English as the Honorary Association of Maritime and River Salvage. This is perhaps somewhat misleading as it is an entirely voluntary organisation almost exclusively concerned with saving life.

Perhaps the word salvage might have been more appropriately translated as 'rescue'.

The association is based on Montevideo and has established rescue stations in suitable positions. Since its foundation, it has been in constant touch with both the RNLI and the German DGzRS. In 1957 the association bought a 48½ ft (14.8 m) lifeboat of the Ramsgate type from the RNLI and this is now stationed at Puerto del Buceo, Montivedeo. An inflatable rescue craft is also maintained at the same station. Crews consist of 21 volunteers divided into 3 groups, maintaining a duty crew at all times. An auxiliary lifeboat is also used.

South Africa

The Department of Transport is responsible for all search and rescue which is controlled by a permanent committee with headquarters in Pretoria (short title PECSAR). A volunteer body, the National Sea Rescue Institute (NSRI) provides inshore rescue services covering the coasts of the Republic. NSRI is state subsidised and comes under the overall control of PECSAR.

The commercial ports of South Africa are state-run and the port captains are allocated areas of responsibility for sea rescue. The ports concerned are Walvis Bay, Ludertiz, Port Nolloth, Cape Town, Mossel Bay, Port Elizabeth and Durban.

NSRI establish inshore rescue stations where needed and at present there are 20 lifeboats in commission from Saldanha Bay on the south-west coast to Richards Bay north of Durban. Rescue operations are co-ordinated by port captains. In addition, the South African Navy have a permanent crash boat station at Saldanha Bay and operate small craft for sea rescue at Simonstown.

In commercial ports there are about 17 large and 13 small tugs available for rescue work. NSRI operate one German built seagoing lifeboat based on Durban with 14 fast rescue boats of the 16½ ft (5 m) class and two of the 33 ft (10 m) class from their various stations. The RSA Navy operates three 96 ft (29.3 m) crash boats based on Saldanha Bay and two tugs from Simonstown.

The South African Air Force (SAAF) operates Shackleton aircraft for long-range duty and various types of helicopters for coastal work. In association with NSRI a helicopter firm at Cape Town and a firm operating Cesna aircraft for whale spotting from Durban provide search and rescue services on the coast on a completely voluntary basis.

During the year ended March 1972, the SAAF carried out 4 rescue operations and the Navy 3. NSRI answered 176 calls for assistance and saved 50 lives and 44 vessels and boats. Crews of state vessels are full-time employees and NSRI crews are volunteers and at immediate call twenty-four hours a day.

NSRI, which was registered in June 1967 as a non-profit

Rescue craft *Natal Nomad* of the National Sea Rescue Institute of South Africa. Stationed at Durban the boat, the Hartley type has a length of 19½ ft (6 m), speed of 35 knots and a range of 90 miles at 20 knots.

making organisation, obviously relieves the state services of a great deal of responsibility for sea rescue and is yet another illustration of the value and efficiency of voluntary work in this sector.

Copies of the NSRI *News Review* give details of many fine rescues and illustrates the importance of this spirited organisation, particularly in dealing with local casualties. A complex operation carried out by NSRI station No. 10 (Simonstown) in conjunction with station No. 2 (Bakoven) and local boat clubs shows clearly the efficient organisation and co-operation which has been built up.

On the morning of 11 March 1972 the speed boat *Coral* left Buffels Bay to fish 30 miles west of Cape Point. She failed to return that night and a general alert was called. NSRI instituted a search at daylight next day assisted by the SA Marlin and Tuna club and the Cape Skiboat club. Searching west and north of Hout Bay the fleet was joined by the NSRI rescue boat from Bakoven and two tunny fishing craft. Eventually the missing boat was located by a SAAF Dakota aircraft and the position passed to the NSRI rescue boat which was close at hand.

The newest and largest addition to the NSRI fleet, *Spirit of Safmarine*, on trials off Cape Town in April 1977.

193

In fact, the rescue operation was successfully completed at 02.00 on the 13 March, by which time the NSRI Simonstown boat had covered 380 miles and had been at sea for over 17 hours with the same coxswain, Dennis Linklater. This feat of endurance was matched by Albert Kelly who controlled 20 units by radio continuously for the same period.

Many others were concerned in this operation including the SAAF and Army and the Port Authorities. NSRI station No. 9 (Gordon's Bay) posted look-outs on the cliffs towards Hangklip and it must be doubtful whether the distressed mariners in *Coral* had ever had so much concern shown for their welfare before – or since!

Australia

The early history of Australia is closely linked to the fortunes of the square-rigged sailing vessels which not only brought out the early European settlers but in the beginning kept them supplied with food and other necessities.

Although the coast of New South Wales had its incidents, the comparatively narrow entrance to Sydney Harbour does not appear to have presented any major problems to masters in sail. On the other hand, ships bound for Melbourne had to enter the almost completely landlocked harbour through Port Phillip Heads, with a sharp turn to starboard immediately inside and a nasty race set up by the swirling tide. It must have been a splendid sight to see a full-rigged ship entering as she would have to carry plenty of sail to ensure that she had sufficient way to clear the heads and negotiate the tricky turn inside. Not unexpectedly, there have been many strandings in this dangerous and confined channel. Even powerful modern ships have been in difficulties here so the problems for sailing ships must have been acute. It was therefore an obvious place for a lifeboat and what was probably one of the first in Australia was established just inside the entrance at Queenscliff. This is said to have been in 1856, but an instruction issued to the head pilot at Shortland's

Bluff (Queenscliff) in 1853 placed the lifeboats at the Heads in his charge.

The first boat or boats appear to have been ordinary ship's lifeboats but possibly better equipped. In 1859 a second station was opened at Point Lonsdale, also on the western side of the entrance. This was a twelve-oared boat of improved design and in May 1861 she went to the assistance of the barque *Asa Packer* which struck the Point Nepean reef when beating through the entrance in a westerly gale. After three attempts, the lifeboat got alongside the wreck and saved the whole crew.

A third lifeboat was built at Williamstown to the RNLI Peake design followed by others which were stationed at Warrnambool, Port Fairy, Portland Bay and Port Albert.

The present Queenscliff lifeboat was built at Adelaide by

Victoria, Australia. The Queenscliff lifeboat launching from her station at the entrance to Port Phillip Bay in the approaches to Melbourne. A 45 ft (13.7 m) RNLI Watson design, she was built at Port Adelaide and commenced her service in 1926.

McFarlane's to the RNLI Watson design, 45 ft (13.7 m) long with a 12½ ft (3.8 m) beam. She arrived at her station in April 1926 and is still in service, having been re-engined with a 75 hp Gardner diesel. The manning of the boat is largely traditional, a volunteer group undertaking to provide a crew as required, including two coxswains and two engineers, one of whom is always available. Control is exercised by a superintendent who is the Ports and Harbours lightkeeper at Queenscliff. Of recent years there have not been many calls for assistance other than from yachts and pleasure craft generally, although the steamer *Wangara* grounded off Point Lonsdale in 1961 and the *Karoon* and *Beltana* both struck the

The Queenscliff lifeboat launches for the ceremony of 'Blessing the Fleet' in 1972. She has now been withdrawn from service and may be replaced by an RNLI Waveney class lifeboat.

Corsair reef in 1963 but apparently all three vessels refloated without casualties. The Queenscliff lifeboat also made a protracted search for the late Prime Minister of Australia, Mr H. Holt when he was lost swimming off Cheviot Beach in December 1967. In 1977, this lifeboat was reported as being replaced.

Another early lifeboat was the *City of Adelaide*. She was built of steel and powered by a steam engine with water jet propulsion, so would appear to be of the same design as the British and Dutch steam lifeboats. Probably she was built in Britain and shipped out to Adelaide. She was stationed at Beachport and seems to have had a remarkably quiet existence as her first service was to the steamer *Time* in 1911, fifteen years after her arrival in 1896. She had been presented to the state by Mr R. Barr-Smith and in 1909, when her boiler needed re-tubing, it was decided to replace the steam engine and jet propulsion with a petrol engine and propeller.

Newcastle, New South Wales, was a difficult harbour for sailing ships to enter and many wrecks occurred in the vicinity. Pilots, who normally used whale boats for boarding, were charged with the responsibility of rendering assistance to ships in distress. It would seem then that the first lifeboats here were whale boats or surfboats with a pilot in charge and, as was usual in the pilot service, a crew of convicts. The earliest record of a lifeboat service at Newcastle concerns the rescue of the crew of the cutter *Vulcan*, wrecked on Stockton beach in 1837. A lifeboat was built at Newcastle in 1847 and another was built in Sydney but proved defective. A third boat built in England saw service for many years.

No record has been found of lifeboats in Queensland or Western Australia, but for many years and until quite recently, an ex-lifeboat served as a pilot boat at Fremantle and was no doubt used for rescue work if required.

Out in the Pacific, 300 miles east of Cape Byron, New South Wales, are two isolated dangers to navigation, 30 miles apart. One is called Middleton reef and 30 miles to the southward is Elizabeth reef, a coral formation enclosing a lagoon, the fringes being covered at high water. Over the years, a number of vessels have been wrecked on these reefs and any survivors would be certain to die of thirst or starvation unless rescued by a passing vessel, of which there would be little chance. In 1870, a lifeboat was purchased by public subscription and placed in the lagoon of Elizabeth reef. The boat was provisioned and provided with everything necessary to make the voyage to the Australian mainland. This must surely have been the most isolated and unusual lifeboat in the world, unmanned but certainly capable of saving life. Castaways taking the boat were instructed to leave a message in a float provided, attached to the mooring. This was to consist of an account of the disaster, names of survivors and any people lost, and the course they intended to steer.

Other isolated and uninhabited islands and rocks were at one time provided with shelters and stocks of food but visiting ships usually reported the food as missing; possibly eaten by animals. Today, with world-wide communications it is no doubt assumed that in the event of a disaster survivors would be able to inform a shore station or nearby ships of their plight. Even so there have been recent reports of men having died of exposure, thirst or starvation on uninhabited islets after surviving shipwreck.

Possibly the most interesting feature of life saving in Australia is the number of important volunteer coastguard and rescue groups all round the coast, some of whom receive state grants but which rely principally on donations and subscriptions. Equipment includes high-speed rescue boats, marine ambulances, rocket apparatus and one seaplane is mentioned. Lectures on boating safety are a feature and in some areas regular patrols are carried out. In general it would seem that normal working craft play a large part in sea rescue, backed up by the Royal Australian Navy and Air Force. A number of volunteer organisations deal with calls for assistance to yachts, pleasure craft, swimmers and people indulging in all sorts of water sports. Since such a large proportion of Australians live in the coastal areas and are very sea-minded it is not surprising that the system seems to work very well.

In April 1972 the Minister for Shipping and Transport, Mr Peter Nixon, opened a Marine Operations Centre in Canberra. This has taken the place of the regional centres which previously had been used to co-ordinate search and rescue operations. It is staffed with specialist officers and functions twenty-four hours a day.

Each Australian state is responsible for marine search and rescue within port limits and for yachts, pleasure craft and fishing vessels in near coastal waters. For ships at sea a coastal radio station would pass any distress message to the Marine Operations Centre and alert all ships by auto alarm, repeating the message.

New Zealand

The Sumner Lifeboat Institution was founded near Christchurch in 1898 as a voluntary organisation and it is still a flourishing and efficient service. Originally operating a surfboat in Sumner Bay, the Institution later obtained an ex-RNLI self-righter and named her *Rescue II*. More recently an RNLI Liverpool type lifeboat was obtained and named *Rescue III*. This craft has been completely overhauled and

The Sumner Lifeboat Institution's Liverpool type lifeboat 35½ ft (10.8 m) *Rescue III* with *Aid II*.

fitted with two 32 hp Perkins diesel engines, which were flown out from Britain by the RAF and RNZAF. This looks as if somebody had some friends in the air force! The boat has also been fitted with a Kelvin Hughes radar set and full communication equipment. A fast surf rescue boat *Aid II* is used for inshore work.

The Sumner Institution has assisted in organising a new rescue station at Kaikoura to which *Rescue II* has been transferred. She has been completely overhauled and installed in a modern station built entirely by members of the voluntary Kaikoura Lifeboat Institution. The links with both the old country and the RNLI are clearly apparent.

A new rescue station has recently been opened at Wellington and it is believed that there is another station at Raglan. The voluntary services all work in co-operation with the main New Zealand search and rescue organisation, the Navy and the Air Force.

There are search and rescue co-ordination centres in Auckland, Christchurch and Wellington with rescue vessels at Auckland, Russel, Christchurch, Wanganui, Wellington and Westport.

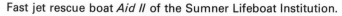

Fast jet rescue boat *Aid II* of the Sumner Lifeboat Institution.

CHAPTER SEVEN

POLAND, USSR, JAPAN, REST OF THE WORLD, INTERNATIONAL LIFEBOAT CONFERENCES

Poland

The responsibility for sea rescue in Poland lies with the Polish Ship Salvage Company (*Polskie Ratownictwo Okretowe*), a state enterprise established in 1951 with its head office in Gdynia. The organisation combines rescue and salvage operations with great success, saving many lives.

The 100ft (30.4 m) Polish rescue and salvage cruiser *Huragan*. Speed 13 knots.

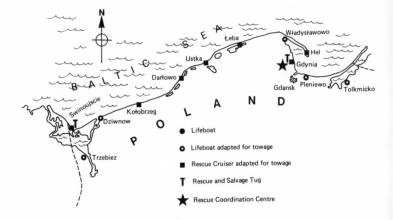

Type and location of sea rescue facilities in Poland.

The Polish coastline is about 360 miles in length and in general the sea bed inshore is sandy and slopes gently so that large ships are rarely in great danger if they ground.

There are 12 rescue and salvage stations on the Polish coast with a co-ordination centre at Gdynia able to alert all available vessels and aircraft in the vicinity of a casualty. Vessels and equipment are constantly brought up to date to meet the requirements of the merchant and fishing fleets. Salvage tugs and vessels of various types including ice-breakers are used, together with lifeboats of about 45 ft (13.7 m) in length.

The rescue stations are situated at Gdynia, Hel, Darlowo, Świnoujscie, Ustka, Kolobrzeg, Wladyslawowo, Leba, Pleniewo, Tolkmicko, Dziwnow, Trzebiez. At the present time 6 rescue cruisers and towage vessels and 6 lifeboats are maintained and there are 6 coastal stations run by Marine Boards and equipped for shore rescue. All operations are controlled from the rescue co-ordination centre at Gdynia which has comprehensive communication equipment.

USSR

The Russian Society for the Preservation of Life from Shipwreck was founded in 1872 and not long afterwards the British residents of St Petersburg (now Leningrad) commissioned two lifeboats to be built at Limehouse in London by the RNLI builders, Forrestt's. These were standard RNLI self-righters, 33 ft long with a beam of 8½ ft. They were offered to the Duke of Edinburgh and the Grand Duchess Marie of Russia as a wedding present and were subsequently stationed at Nicolaiev on the Black Sea and on the island of Oesel in the Baltic. Later, the name of the organisation was changed to the Imperial Russian Life Saving Society. In the early part of this century, the Society relied upon voluntary subscriptions to a large extent but also received an annual grant from the state.

Today, the Soviet Rescue Service is under the control of the Ministry of the Maritime Fleet. It is run by the state and was founded in 1921. It has rescue stations on the Barents, Baltic and Black Seas, and on the Pacific coast. The rescue service is available to render any sort of assistance to ships in addition to life saving and undertakes towing, fire fighting and removal of wrecks. A wide variety of vessels are used including tugs, sea-going and coastal lifeboats, divers' launches and high-speed rescue boats. The rescue service works in close co-operation with other services including the air force, navy, merchant shipping and fishing fleets. The USSR is a signatory to the International Convention for the Safety of Life at Sea.

Many gallant rescues have been carried out by the Soviet service, a great number to ships and vessels of other nations. The USSR has rescue agreements with countries whose waters adjoin theirs: Sweden, Denmark and Finland in the Baltic; Norway for the Barents Sea; Japan for the Pacific. An agreement was signed in 1956 with the Chinese People's Republic and the Korean People's Republic (North Korea) for eastern waters and with the German Democratic Republic (East Germany) and Poland for the Baltic. These agreements provide for assistance and co-ordination be-tween the signatories and call for continuous communication arrangements to deal with distress messages.

In addition to the work of the rescue service, Soviet ships at sea have rendered assistance to vessels of many nations, often at great risk. In one outstanding rescue, the Soviet tanker *Sovetskaya Neft* went to the assistance of a French passenger ship which was on fire. The tanker had a highly inflammable cargo on board and her captain might well have considered the risks involved too great but in fact did not hesitate. In another incident the Norwegian tanker *Folga* was badly on fire but the Soviet ship *Tartu* came to her assistance and rescued her crew at great risk to the lives of the Soviet seamen.

The Emergency Rescue Service of the USSR controls upwards of 200 motor lifeboats, 3,000 pulling boats and a number of rescue cruisers. In addition a fleet of salvage vessels and ice-breakers is used in rescue operations. It may be noted that the Soviet authorities consider that the most reasonable way of saving people in distress at sea is to save the ship which they are on.

China

It has been suggested that China was in fact the first country with an organised sea, or at any rate river, rescue service, with lifeboats stationed on the Yangtse River, up-stream from Shanghai. In his *Book of the Life-boat*, published in 1909, A. L. Haydon says there were 200 lifeboats at more than 100 stations. They are described as of junk design, built of pine and from 35 ft to 45 ft in length, the larger ones having a crew of six. It is also interesting to note that it is said that unlike most services the boatmen were not expected to salvage property but were strictly confined to saving life.

The year 1737 has been suggested as the possible date of the start of the Chinese rescue service but as one cynical commentator put it, 'The Chinese always do claim to have invented everything, from gunpowder to civilisation'. However, there is no doubt that the country did get a head start in many spheres and it would be churlish to deny that great nation the distinction of being the first to organise a river rescue service.

Adjacent to the coast of China, rescue craft are stationed in Korea, the Sea of Okhotsk, Hong Kong and the Philippines, but precise details of rescue craft and stations in China itself are regrettably lacking. Attempts to obtain official information may or may not bear fruit at some future date.

Japan

With its long, irregular coastline and liability to sudden violent changes of weather, it is perhaps not surprising that Japan has a high average marine accident rate of over 3,000 casualties a year. Most of the vessels involved are small, and fishing craft predominate. There are in fact over 400,000 vessels engaged in fishing in Japanese waters.

The Japanese islands are of volcanic origin and have many narrow channels with a great number of harbours, many modern factories having specially constructed ports of their own. A large percentage of accidents take place in these narrow channels and there have been some serious collisions resulting in ships sinking and lives being lost. But by far the greater number of casualties involved fishing craft, with stranding and engine trouble the principal causes.

As Japan is in the typhoon area this is yet another hazard, particularly for the smaller craft. One of the most violent of these storms occurred in 1959 when typhoon 'Isewan' hit the Tokai area of central Japan at midnight on 26 September. Losses and damage to houses, shore installations and vessels were immense and more than 5,000 lives were lost. It was the worst typhoon ever recorded and the strains placed on the rescue services were intolerable.

The Imperial Society for Saving and Succouring the Shipwrecked was founded in 1889 and in choosing such a lengthy title was merely following the example of the European organisations of the time. In 1903 Count de Yashu,

Jet-propelled inshore rescue boat of the Japanese NSK organisation for operation in shallow water.

president of the society, notified the Spanish life saving organisation that it was proposed to model the Japanese service on their lines. Both were voluntary societies but in receipt of some state aid.

Today, the *Nippon Suinan Kyusaikai*, the Japanese Life Saving Institute, has 459 rescue stations and branches with about 18,000 members. This again is a voluntary institution aided by municipal grants, as local authorities are required by law to provide assistance to aircraft and vessels in distress in their areas.

All rescue activities concerned with marine casualties are under the control of the Marine Safety Board (MSB) of the Japanese Government which has search and rescue aircraft and vessels stationed at bases throughout Japan. The MSB attaches great importance to the support and encouragement of the Life Saving Institute and arranges instruction in rescue techniques for its members, also lending rescue

Training of NSK rescue personnel — line-throwing rocket firing exercise.

Use of dummy for training NSK crews in mouth-to-mouth resuscitation.

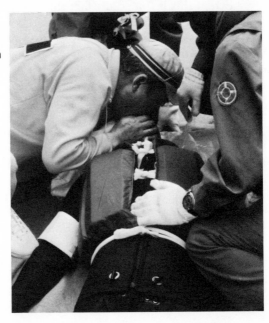

equipment without charge. A recent survey shows that rescue operations were successful in 70 per cent of cases and of the total number the MSB were responsible for 60 per cent and the Life Saving Institute for 18 per cent with private craft or individuals dealing with the remainder.

The combination of a state and a voluntary organisation has resulted in an extensive, efficient and carefully co-ordinated rescue service based on modern technology.

The Guard and Rescue Department of the Maritime Safety Agency controls 308 lifeboats of various designs. The voluntary organisation *Nippon Suinan Kyusaikai* has 48 lifeboats and 29 inshore rescue boats.

The rest of the world

It has no doubt been noted that the sea rescue arrangements already described, although extensive, only deal with a com-paratively small portion of the surface of the world. To a large extent this is due to the fact that thousands of miles of coastline are wild and uninhabited and coastal shipping is virtually non-existent. Local fishing fleets and the occasional vessel which might pass that way would hardly warrant the establishment of a costly rescue station – even if the local authority came to consider such a thing and men could be found to man it. Sea rescue originated in busy waters, natur-ally tending to expand with increasing trade, and latterly with greater use of coastal waters for recreation. In the days of the large inshore fishing fleets, there were lifeboats at nearly every town and village from which the boats put out, and no doubt the fishermen looked upon them as a necessary insurance. Indeed, at one time the lifeboats relied almost entirely on inshore fishermen for their crews.

Even today, on the long stretches of raw coastline, and far out on the great oceans, distressed seamen must still rely on their own exertions or the chance proximity of another vessel for survival. Nearly every nation requires the masters of its vessels to render what assistance they can to a vessel in distress; there have been few suggestions of seamen failing in their obligations to anyone in distress at sea. Modern communications have minimised the dangers of disaster at sea and the AMVER* system has gone a long way towards perfecting rescue co-ordination in mid-ocean.

Sources of information

Attempts to obtain information about sea rescue organisation direct from the country concerned are not always successful. In Britain it would be natural to turn to the Royal Navy, Lloyd's of London and the civil air lines, all of whom might be interested in mounting a rescue operation in distant waters. From these three sources a great deal of information on rescue at sea may be obtained, although quite a lot of this is of a negative character, particularly where the availability of lifeboats is concerned.

The British Admiralty 'Pilots' or 'Sailing Directions' consist of 73 volumes describing for the navigator the coasts of the world in considerable detail. Indexed under 'Life-saving services' in each volume will be found information on the sea rescue arrangements, including lifeboats and line-throwing apparatus, in the area covered. A careful study of all the volumes leads to the conclusion that there is indeed much of the world where there is no sea rescue organisation of the type that has been described. This does not mean that there are no rescue arrangements at all but does mean that when necessary the work is probably carried out by ordinary working craft such as pilot boats, harbour launches and so on, backed up by any naval or air force facilities available. For example, an extract from an Indian Notice to Mariners gives details of distress communication arrangements and defines the four sectors into which the coast of India is divided for search and rescue purposes. Each of these has its joint operations room which acts as rescue co-ordinating centre. Ships

---

* Automated Mutual Assistance Vessel Rescue, by which a computer keeps track of vessels on passage so that the nearest ship can be alerted in the case of the vessel needing assistance.

and aircraft of the Indian Navy and Air Force are used for rescue work and presumably smaller craft under ports and harbours jurisdiction also. This system is probably very similar to that in use in other countries which do not have a separate rescue or life saving organisation, of which there are still quite a number.

The ICAO

Another source of information, more particularly on search and rescue for aircraft but also of interest to surface craft is the International Civil Aviation Organisation. This body has its headquarters in Ottawa, Canada, and publishes five volumes of regional air navigation plans giving complete details of the search and rescue arrangements for the whole world. These embrace all regular air routes and involve the use of short, medium and long range aircraft, and helicopters, for rescue work. Two types of surface rescue craft are listed, one described as suitable for inshore work and the other for offshore work. The maps showing the rescue centres and the areas covered by their available rescue facilities add very considerably to the information on life saving arrangements throughout the world, particularly in areas where apparently no purely surface rescue organisation exists.

The International Lifeboat Conference

As the boats and equipment for sea rescue became more sophisticated and techniques more involved, the need for international exchange of ideas and experience became increasingly apparent. The Breton Society had previously held meetings in France, attended by delegates from other nations, but what is now known as the first International Lifeboat Conference was held in London in 1924, the centenary of the founding of the National Institution for the Preservation of Life from Shipwreck by Sir William Hillary. This institution eventually changed its name and became the RNLI, the body which organised the conference in 1924.

It was decided that invitations to the first conference

should be limited to countries 'known to possess an organised lifeboat service' and it would now appear that a somewhat narrow interpretation was given to this condition. Only ten invitations were issued, and eight countries (Denmark, France, Netherlands, Norway, Sweden, Spain, the USA and Japan) accepted. Germany and Portugal regretted that financial considerations prevented their attendance.

There was a modest but interesting agenda and six foreign lifeboats came over and were berthed in the River Thames with two British boats. All were open to the public and a cruise was made in company up river to Fulham. The deliberations were held in Westminster City Hall and a great deal of attention was given to the fitting of internal combustion engines, still very much on trial in lifeboats. In the course of these discussions, Mr F. Rubie, surveyor of lifeboats to the RNLI and designer of the Rubie self-righter, produced a rather surprising piece of information. This was that 12 men pulling oars only produced a total of 2–3 hp and that the sails of a sailing lifeboat could produce 50 hp. The delegates were fully convinced of the ability of an engine to increase the efficiency of a lifeboat, but they also realised that it produced a whole host of new problems.

There was also a certain amount of social activity and no doubt some interesting discussions outside the conference hall. Lifeboat crews were taken to the Wembley Exhibition and there was a celebration dinner at the Hotel Cecil at which the Prince of Wales presided. Delegates were strongly impressed with the value of the conference and it was decided to hold further meetings at intervals of four years, a different country playing host each time.

The second conference was held in Paris in 1928. On this occasion, eighteen nations submitted papers and seventeen attended the meetings. Those taking part were Belgium, Britain, Denmark, Finland, France, Germany, Greece, Netherlands, Italy, Japan, Latvia, Poland, Spain, Sweden, Turkey, the USA and the USSR. Motor lifeboats were still the main subject of discussion and apparently still something of a novelty. This is quite surprising, as by 1928 most passenger ships of any size carried at least one motor lifeboat. Tunnels for propellers, particularly in twin-screw boats, were occupying the attention of both France and Britain.

The symbol of the International Lifeboat Conference. Between conferences the ILC has a permanent base at the RNLI Headquarters in Poole, England.

The conferences, now well established, continued up to the outbreak of World War II and were re-established in 1947 with a conference in Norway, after which Belgium and Portugal were, in turn, the host countries. In 1959, the conference was held in Bremen at the invitation of the Lifeboat Institution of the German Federal Republic (DGzRS) and lifeboats and rescue cruisers from many countries were available for inspection. The RNLI sent a new 52 ft (15.8 m) Barnett type lifeboat which called at Ramsgate, Den Helder and Borkum, the round trip being something over 1,000 miles. One of the most interesting features of this conference was a demonstration of twenty or more lifejackets by a team of expert swimmers. The behaviour of some of these 'life-jackets' was such that it was as well that the swimmers were indeed experts. The results were illuminating but hardly reassuring.

In 1963 it became Britain's turn once more and a highly successful conference was held in Edinburgh, with many visiting lifeboats of advanced design berthed in Leith docks and some interesting displays put on for the general public.

In 1967 the conference was held in Dinard with France as host and in 1971 the delegates crossed the Atlantic to the USA, where the tremendous changes in design of recent years were clearly emphasised and the great US Coast Guard organisation admired and perhaps secretly envied. The arrangements and discussions of the various conferences are of absorbing interest to any student of sea rescue but unfortunately quite beyond the scope of this book. Perhaps one day they will be the subject of a volume of their own.

CHAPTER EIGHT

LIFEBOAT DISASTERS

Whenever an accident occurs to a lifeboat and members of her crew are lost, there is an immediate outcry of 'Why was this allowed to happen?' The inference is that a lifeboat should be so designed and constructed that she is proof against any dangers that sea rescue may involve. Some of the best naval architects in the world, with access to many years of lifeboat experience, have tried to achieve that desirable aim. So far, all these efforts have failed and there seems every likelihood that they will continue to do so. It is perhaps strange that other accidents involving greater loss of life happen daily without any outcry from the press or public at all.

When people at sea are in dire peril of losing their lives, to rescue them is rarely easy or safe. When a ship or yacht is aground on a sandbank or rocky shore the hazards are considerable. The men involved in effecting a rescue are well aware of this fact and it is no doubt generally accepted that the admiration for lifeboatmen is centred upon their bravery even more than upon their skill and seamanship.

Over the years, by far the greater proportion of the work of lifeboats has been carried out in shallow water, close inshore. That is where vessels most often become casualties and where immediate assistance becomes vital. Distress in deep water, though by no means unknown, is a comparative rarity in lifeboat operations. A ship with a shifting cargo or the victim of fire or explosion at sea may be anywhere on the oceans of the world, and possibly far out of range of any lifeboat or even aircraft. It is therefore quite reasonable to expect that the number of calls for lifeboat assistance in deep water would be less than those inshore. It is for this reason that a lifeboat must have a shallow draught. The design must be a compromise between the best sea-keeping characteristics and the ability to meet the wide variety of duties which a lifeboat may be called upon to perform.

Theoretically, any craft will capsize if given the necessary conditions, and apart from giving a lifeboat the maximum stability for her draught, there is not much that a designer can do about it. Not every craft will return to her normal position after a capsize and the early self-righters were designed to give the crews a better chance if the boat did go right over. But the very fact of building the self-righting quality into the boat made her less easy to handle and indeed more prone to capsize. This does *not* apply to the modern self-righter which relies on the transfer of water ballast or watertight superstructure to prevent her remaining in the capsized position. It has been said that the modern self-righter is not as good a boat as she would be without the self-righting arrangements, but once again, compromises have to be made and absolute perfection is yet to be achieved. (Since the foregoing was written the RNLI has now designed and built a new type of self-righter which does not rely on the transfer of water ballast.)

Britain

The loss of the Mumbles, South Wales, lifeboat in April 1947 was one of the worst disasters in the history of the RNLI, for in addition to the 8 man crew of the lifeboat all 41 members of the crew of the ship she had gone to assist were drowned. This was the *Samtampa*, a vessel of 7,000 tons, bound for Newport, Monmouthshire, in ballast.

'Flying light', with a gale force wind on her quarter, the ship was not steering well as she made her way up the Bristol Channel and when she began to close the land the situation became serious. With the ship virtually out of control, her master decided to anchor, but it soon became clear that her ground tackle would not hold and calls for assistance were sent by radio.

Having received the message, soon after 18.00 that evening, the Mumbles lifeboat launched into a high breaking sea with fierce squalls and poor visibility. Just as she left, a further message was received and the boat returned to within hailing distance and was given a new position for the casualty. Coxswain William Gammon waved acknowledgement and once more the 45 ft (13.7 m) Watson lifeboat plunged away on her mission to Sker Point on the other side of the bay. Her gallant crew were not seen alive again.

While the lifeboat was on her way, the *Samtampa* met her end. One cable parted and with the other anchor dragging the ship struck the rocky ledge of Sker Point. The Coastguard rescue team were on the spot but were unable to reach the ship with their rockets. A large number of spectators who had arrived in cars watched helplessly. Then the ship broke into three parts. The centre section, with all hands sheltering on it, sank in deep water, taking the unlucky crew with it. The bow and stern sections drove up on the rocky shore together and when boarded the crews quarters were found to be quite dry. But not a man was saved. Such are the odd quirks of disaster.

Next morning, the lifeboat was found on the rocks as the tide receded, bottom up and with the bodies of her crew round about her.

No one knows what caused the disaster to the lifeboat, but it is probable that on arrival at the scene William Gammon decided to close the vessel, or what he could see of her. With the high, breaking sea rebounding from the rocky ledges huge, unpredictable waves must have overwhelmed the lifeboat, driving her ashore beside the remains of the vessel she had come to assist.

The Mayor of Swansea opened a fund for the dependants of the lifeboat crew and pensions were granted by the RNLI. The fund soon reached a total of £91,000. A new crew volunteered at once and manned a reserve lifeboat which was sent to the station. A new lifeboat for the Mumbles was built and called the *William Gammon*. This was a gift of the

Civil Service and Post Office Lifeboat Fund.

The Mumbles lifeboat, a fine, able craft, was lost in attempting what must have been a virtually impossible rescue from seaward. The fact that an attempt was made, and of that there can be little doubt, emphasises the determined heroism of Coxswain Gammon and his crew who cannot have failed to realise the odds against them.

Should the lifeboat have been sent on such a mission? The answer is certainly 'yes', since at the time of the call no one really knew what the possibilities of rescue were or would be like when the lifeboat arrived on the scene. The final decision on the spot has to rest with the coxswain in all such cases and he is under no obligation to attempt the impossible. But having been sent to try and effect a rescue he would probably have no illusions as to the possibility of criticism if he did not at least make an effort. Without radio communication with the shore he could not even share the responsibility. Today, since all lifeboats have radio telephony, it should be possible for those on shore in an executive position to prevent a coxswain being faced with a situation in which he may be persuaded to sign the death warrant of himself and his crew.

Prior to the Mumbles disaster, the last occasion on which a RNLI lifeboat was lost with all hands was in November 1928 on the south coast of England at Rye harbour, Sussex. The pulling and sailing boat stationed there capsized in the surf with the loss of the 17 men in her crew. Nearly every family in the small village was bereaved. From then until the loss of the Mumbles boat, there were 5 other capsizes in which altogether 20 lives were lost, 5 of them survivors from a wreck. Three of the boats were self-righters. Since 1947, 8 lifeboats have capsized, 3 of them with the loss of all hands. Two of these 8 boats were self-righters. In every case except one, the capsize occurred at or near a harbour entrance or near the shore in heavy breaking water. The only instance of a lifeboat capsizing in open sea was that of the Fraserburgh boat in January 1970 and in spite of the detailed inquiry into her loss it is still a matter of conjecture as to how or why this happened. The suggestion that the Watson type lifeboats were unsuitable to face the rigours of a winter North Sea gale can only have been made by someone without seagoing experience in these boats. But the Fraserburgh lifeboat had been re-engined and her stability and trim had altered in the process. Although it was said that this was not a contributory cause of the disaster there seems a possibility that indirectly it may have triggered off a chain of events.

USA

Although perhaps the RNLI has had more than its share of accidents to lifeboats in the last twenty-five years, other countries have had their losses also. At 17.00 on the afternoon of 12 January 1961, the lifeboat station at Point Adams on the coast of Oregon, USA, was requested to send their 52 ft (15.8 m) lifeboat *Triumph* to the assistance of the fishing vessel *Mermaid*, in difficulties on the Columbia River bar, having lost her rudder. A 40 ft (12.2 m) and a 36 ft (11 m) lifeboat were already on the spot, but were unable to take the *Mermaid* in tow owing to the adverse conditions. The wind was south-south-east at 55 knots and there was a heavy breaking sea on the bar.

The *Triumph* managed to get the *Mermaid* in tow and was proceeding slowly in shore when the towrope parted. In turning to attempt to pass another towrope *Triumph* was hit by a heavy breaker and capsized. Of her crew of six, one man managed to swim to the *Mermaid* and another remained in the lifeboat which drove ashore later and righted herself in the process.

About the same time, the 40 ft lifeboat which was standing by to assist in the vicinity of the bar was also struck by a great breaking sea and capsized. The 36 ft boat, also standing by, was able to rescue all the crew of three of the 40 ft boat, despite the fact that she herself had had a stern compartment flooded in the same breakers. With his craft in this disabled condition the coxswain managed to get alongside the

Columbia River lightship to which everyone on board transferred. The 36 ft boat was moored up astern of the lightship but later the mooring rope parted and she was lost.

Meanwhile another 36 ft lifeboat had arrived on the scene and had managed to take the *Mermaid* in tow, but once more the towrope parted. The visibility was very poor and this time the fishing vessel was almost immediately lost to sight in the darkness and driving spume. She was never seen again and her crew of two and the survivor from *Triumph* who swam to her after the capsize were lost.

Of the crew of six of the *Triumph*, only one, Gordon Huggins, survived. He was the man who remained on board through the capsize and when the lifeboat righted herself close inshore, he jumped into the breakers and fought his way to the beach, where he was found in a shocked condition. Thus the total casualties amounted to five men from the *Triumph* and the crew of two of the *Mermaid*, together with the 40 ft and 36 ft lifeboats, both of which sank. The crew of three of the 36 ft boat and the three survivors from the 40 ft boat undoubtedly owed their lives to the decision of the coxswain to make at once for the lightship and put everyone on board.

This difficult service, in the dangerous conditions always found on a river or harbour bar in heavy weather is typical of the work a lifeboat is so often called upon to perform and emphasises the necessity for shallow draught. There is also no doubt that the service also emphasised the ability and seagoing qualities of the US Coast Guard 36 ft lifeboat.

Netherlands

Just over fifty years ago, the Dutch lifeboat *Brandaris* foundered with the loss of all hands. On the night of Saturday 22 October 1921, a fierce gale sprang up and raged with unabated ferocity over the whole weekend, ending as suddenly as it began with a spell of fine summery weather. The Sunday was a day of disaster with force 10–11 winds and many ships in trouble. The steam lifeboat *President van Heel* at the Hook of Holland, put to sea to the assistance of a French vessel in distress, capsized at the entrance to the New Waterway and stranded on the south pier. Six out of her crew of seven were lost, although the lifeboat was subsequently salved and continued in service for some years.

From all round the coast came reports of ships in difficulties, amongst them the German schooner *Liesbeth* of 141 tons, bound for Gothenburg with a cargo of English china clay from Fowey in Cornwall. She had reached the East Goodwin lightship in the North Sea at noon on 22 October, and with a south-west gale behind her, made rapid progress towards the German Bight under storm canvas. Approaching the Dutch coast on Sunday night, the master of the *Liesbeth* realised that his ship was making a lot of leeway and would not weather the banks off the island of Texel, so he decided that the only chance was to run for the Engelsmans Gat between Texel and Vlieland. In what must have been a breathtaking sail, the *Liesbeth* headed for the gap in the breakers surrounded by broken water and angry seas. It was difficult to determine the channel and she was probably still making leeway for, suddenly, she struck the unyielding Stanley Reef, about 2 miles from the Eirland lighthouse. The situation was terrifying, with heavy seas lifting and bumping the stranded vessel over the sands and crashing on her decks so that the crew had to take to the rigging to avoid being washed overboard. Their distress signals were seen on shore and the pulling lifeboat at Cocksdorp was launched immediately.

It was near low water and for the first part of the lifeboat's journey there was some shelter from the banks, but the last few hundred yards taxed the oarsmen to their utmost and it took them an hour to force the boat through the steep, short seas. When they did reach the casualty, the lifeboat was swamped by a big breaker and driven away to leeward, which meant another long struggle before they got back to the ship. Eventually, they did so and the six men who formed the crew of the *Liesbeth* quickly slid down ropes and were grasped by their rescuers. With wind and sea astern, the lifeboat returned safely to her station. All the crew of the Cocksdorp lifeboat were later decorated for their gallantry and the German government presented each man with a silver watch.

Meanwhile the *Brandaris*, the largest and fastest lifeboat in the Netherlands, and probably in the world at that time, left Terschelling harbour to go to the assistance of the *Liesbeth* also, in case the Cocksdorp boat under oars should be unable to reach the casualty. The crew of the *Brandaris* were fine seamen with plenty of experience of the dangerous waters they had to face. They had full confidence in their well-tried vessel which had a well-established reputation for sea-worthiness.

The people of Terschelling gathered near the lighthouse and watched the lifeboat battling her way along the channel out to sea. The people of Vlieland saw her near the signal station, nearly two hours after her departure. She had then almost completed the worst part of her journey, it was thought. Yet she and her crew were never seen again. Somewhere between the signal station and the wreck of the *Liesbeth*, disaster must have come with terrifying suddenness, but how and in what circumstances no one will ever know. The coxswain, Steven Wiegman, engineer Ferdinand Kies and able-seamen Albert Tot and Rink Dijkstra joined the brotherhood of lifeboatmen who have given their lives in an attempt to save others.

For some time no alarm was felt, but when news of the rescue of the German crew by the Cocksdorp boat came through, an anxious search of the coast was made and the still stormy waters scanned by many worried eyes. The parents, wives and children of the lifeboat crew stayed awake, hoping to hear the footsteps of the returning seamen; but there was just the noise of the storm, the howling of the wind and the rattle of hail on the window panes.

There were some reports of possible sightings of the *Brandaris*, but all proved to be false and the lifeboat was never found. She was a fine, powerful boat, fully tested at an exercise not long before the disaster. The report of the Shipping Council which inquired into her loss said:

'The council is unable to establish the cause of the loss of the *Brandaris* through lack of evidence. In any rescue operation in stormy weather at sea there is always an element of danger. However, the *Brandaris* was adequately equipped to carry out such missions, she was well maintained and had a skilled crew especially trained for rescue service.'

The report ended with a tribute to the lost crew.

Germany

The German rescue cruiser *Adolph Bermpohl*, stationed at Heligoland, sailed at 15.00 on 23 February 1967 on service to the fishing vessel *J. C. Wriede* in distress, 45 miles north-west of the island. At this time, there was a westerly gale force 11, with heavy hurricane force squalls and a westerly storm sea with wave heights exceeding 20 feet (6 m).

About an hour after she sailed, the rescue cruiser was instructed by radio to alter course to a position 8 miles north of Heligoland, where a Dutch fishing vessel *Burgemeester van Kampen* was reported to be in a sinking condition. Other ships were in the vicinity of the *J. C. Wriede* and were preparing to render assistance.

The rescue cruiser reached the Dutch vessel at 17.13 and after assessing the situation, the coxswain decided to launch his small rescue craft, known as the 'daughter boat', to take off the crew of three. At 18.19, the *Adolph Bermpohl* reported that the daughter boat had taken the three men off the fishing vessel but that it was impossible to get her back aboard the rescue cruiser, so both craft would proceed slowly back to harbour together. From that time on, no further communication took place between the shore station and the rescue cruiser, although attempts were made from shore at frequent intervals.

On 24 February 1967 at 09.25, the *Adolph Bermpohl* was found by the motor ship *Atlantis* to the north of the lightship

Elbe I and another rescue cruiser was sent to tow her to Cuxhaven. The daughter boat *Vegesack* was later found capsized. No members of the crew of the rescue craft were found, nor were any of the crew of the Dutch fishing vessel and it was assumed that all had met their deaths by drowning.

Both the *Adolph Bermpohl* and her daughter boat were damaged, mostly in the superstructure, and had it not been for a sharp look-out kept by the Heligoland lighthouse keeper, there would have been no other evidence from which to deduce the cause of the disaster.

The lighthouse keeper reported that at about 18.45, he observed between two heavy squalls the lights of a small vessel in the entrance to the north harbour. He noted that the vessel apparently had a searchlight trained over the side. Two of the light buoys marking the entrance channel had been extinguished by the storm and one was badly out of position. At the subsequent inquiry it was suggested that for some reason not now apparent, the coxswain of the rescue cruiser had decided to risk using the north entrance which was considered highly dangerous in severe weather conditions. Having made this decision, he was apparently going to take the men out of the daughter boat and was in the process of doing this when all were overwhelmed and swept away by a plunging breaker on the sandbank to which they were dangerously close. It would seem that the men aboard the cruiser were assisting those in the daughter boat to transfer to her in the heavy breaking sea, so that all were on deck when the towering wave threw the vessel on her beam ends and carried the lifeboatmen and the Dutch fishermen to their deaths.

It is probable that the coxswain of the *Adolph Bermpohl* decided to risk the north entry in what he knew were dangerous conditions because of his concern for the men in the daughter boat and the necessity to get them to shelter as soon as possible. Examination of both the rescue cruiser and daughter boat, after they had been salvaged, showed that they were both still in full operational condition and that the disaster was not caused by any failure of material or equipment. There was little doubt also that the very experienced crew of the rescue craft acted correctly in every way and whatever decisions the coxswain made were justified by the severe weather and other factors obtaining at the time. These men lived up to the highest ideals of lifeboatmen of all countries and died in their efforts to save others.

* * *

Most of the lifeboat services of the world have suffered losses of men and boats at one time or another, and in view of the great risks involved, it would be remarkable if they had not. The incidents related in this chapter are but a tiny piece of the more tragic history of the sea rescue service but seamen will perhaps discern a linking thread running through them all and the non-technical reader will not fail to be impressed by the humanity and courage of lifeboatmen, whatever their nationality or creed.

CHAPTER NINE

CONCLUSIONS

The human contribution

The outstanding feature of the sea rescue services of the world is the extraordinary dedication and self-sacrifice of the crews of life saving craft. This applies to volunteers and full-time men alike and in this context the distinction is possibly invidious. Bravery and the acceptance of major discomforts are no less praiseworthy because they happen in the course of earning a living; but the fact that so many men of all nations come forward eagerly to take such risks for the satisfaction of saving other men's lives makes nonsense of the violent discords which bedevil human relations today. No doubt one tends to offset the other, but viewed together they make a strange pattern of human behaviour!

Although originally composed of inshore fishermen to a very large extent, today lifeboat crews in most countries form an interesting cross-section of the whole community. Probably most of them have been to sea at some time or other, but the war-time sailors are beginning to show their age and there is a growing tendency for young men with sailing and boating experience to be accepted in crews. And very good lifeboatmen most of them become.

There can be few trades or professions not represented in a lifeboat crew somewhere or other. The records show butchers, bakers, chemists, doctors (often in a dual role), miners, parsons (although some crews say they unlucky in a boat), policemen, publicans, solicitors, town clerks and town hall staff and at least one undertaker. One coxswain even reported that on return from a service he found that one of his crew was a missing patient from a mental home. He said he was a very good seaman! Whatever they do for a living these

225

men have one thing in common, the brotherhood of the sea. It would be wrong to suppose that they are all actuated by the same high ideals or that they are all bluff, kindly seadogs. There are some very tough and gruff seamen amongst them. But one and all are prepared to risk disappointment, discomfort and even death in their efforts to render assistance to those in distress at sea. Such men cannot but command unstinted admiration.

Voluntary and state-run organisations

If the RNLI in Britain were taken over and run by the state, the attitude of the present volunteer crews would be almost certain to change considerably. Nearly all people who work for the state expect to get paid for their efforts. For every lifeboat to have a paid, full-time crew would not be feasible since the average number of services per boat only works out at about seven or eight a year. A full-time crew would be bored with little more than general maintenance, cleaning and polishing to occupy their time. In any case RNLI crews have made it quite clear that they prefer the existing system.

At the same time it is true that what is almost certainly the largest sea rescue organisation in the world, the US Coast Guard, is run by the state and relies on enlisted men for crews of lifeboats and other rescue craft with great success. The short answer is that the US Coast Guard is a very large force engaged in a wide range of activities and with highly trained, disciplined men. From the thousands of men available it must clearly be possible to select men who have a leaning towards lifeboat work or to encourage them to come forward. It would hardly be possible to institute a similar system in Britain as there is no comparable organisation with sufficient manpower. That is with the possible exception of the Royal Navy and it is unlikely that that service would wish to add to its present responsibilities for life saving.

The fact that the responsibility for sea rescue in Britain is to a large extent shared by the Coastguard and the RNLI has already been mentioned but in order to make any comparisons with a wholly state-run system such as the USCG some further details are necessary.

The Coastguard service in Britain is almost entirely a land force and is organised in ten divisions, each of which is sub-divided into three districts. An inspector is in charge of each division, assisted by three district officers who work from coastguard rescue headquarters (CRHQ). There are 150 coastguard stations manned by regular coastguards and 225 auxiliary stations. The force consists of 594 regular coastguards and about 8,800 part-time auxiliaries, most of whom are members of the rescue companies which man the line-throwing equipment. In 1970 a report on the marine search and rescue organisation of the United Kingdom was issued by HM Stationery Office. In this booklet, the functions of the Coastguard and RNLI were described in some detail and their joint responsibility for the 800 privately owned boats enrolled in the special Inshore Rescue Scheme explained. Having pointed out the possibility of objections in theory to a divided command, it was stated that none had been found in practice. Finally the report stated that 'the two services work in the closest collaboration and we can see no virtue in merging them'. It is to be hoped that these wise words continue to be heeded.

In the same report the part played in sea rescue by the Ministry of Defence and the use of ships and aircraft of the Royal Navy and Royal Air Force are also described. It says that the Coastguard can request the appropriate Commander-in-Chief to institute a search for a casualty and the C-in-C can ask the RAF to carry out an air search. Surface craft are under the control of the navy and as naval and air staff both operate at the same maritime headquarters co-ordination presents no problems. The report then gives details of available aircraft and their bases but no doubt the situation has since altered.

Helicopters and inflatables
There were significant changes which affected sea rescue

following the end of World War II. The first was the deployment of the helicopter and its increasing use for life saving. The next was the tremendous increase in the number of people indulging in seafaring sports all over the world. This produced a requirement for speedy rescue facilities in many places not served by conventional lifeboat stations, principally during the months when sea sports are popular.

Helicopters proved far too costly to build and maintain for voluntary organisations to provide them, so that in nearly every country this became a state responsibility. But the fast inshore rescue work, which at one time looked like becoming entirely a helicopter prerogative, was later to a large extent taken over by the inflatable craft driven by an outboard motor. Intensive trials and experiments with inflatable hulls have now produced sophisticated, high-speed craft with rigid bottoms which no doubt are much more expensive and almost certainly not so easy to launch. It remains to be seen whether the increased speed and seaworthiness will out-weigh in value the simplicity and economy of the original craft.

Both the helicopter and the inflatable boat are extremely well suited to the work of inshore rescue. The former more or less by chance, the latter by design. The helicopter's official function as a rescue craft in Britain was to save airmen who have come down in the sea. Hoisting swimmers, dinghy sailors and other seafarers up into the sky from their chosen element was really a sideline and took second place in air–sea rescue priorities. Nevertheless, it is considered that the helicopter must remain an essential part of the sea rescue service and that if navy and air force machines are with-drawn some means of replacing them would have to be found.

Public participation

All charitable institutions have to endure a certain amount of criticism from well-meaning but often misguided people and the press and it may be that this helps to keep them up to scratch. Lifeboat organisations are particularly susceptible and at regular intervals the fact that crews are virtually unpaid is paraded as monstrous. After a disaster there are nearly always suggestions that the lifeboat was probably not fit for the job and that had the service been backed by the resources of the state, the accident would never have occurred. Neither of these criticisms have ever been supported by facts. And when at last it is decided to close a lifeboat station that has been redundant for a number of years, everyone tends to side with the understandably upset local inhabitants without any consideration of the necessity for efficient management or the waste of money involved in maintaining an unnecessary lifeboat.

It will have been noted that in the majority of countries where the sea rescue service is run by the state there is also some participation by volunteers, usually boat owners and yachtsmen. In the USA, the Coast Guard has promoted a volunteer, non-military organisation, the Coast Guard Auxiliary. This force was established by Congress to promote safety in recreational boating and has upwards of 30,000 members, both men and women, including experienced boatmen, amateur radio operators and licensed aircraft pilots. Members' own craft must be equipped to high standards of safety which far exceed the requirements of Federal law.

The Coast Guard Auxiliary carries out three basic programmes: a voluntary motor boat examination; public education in boating safety; operational duties. This last includes patrol work at regattas and rescue work. All these are frequently carried out in conjunction with regular Coast Guard units. The details of the activities of the Auxiliary in 1970 are impressive:

Non-members instructed in safe boating courses	209,521
Motor boats examined	236,718
Cases of assistance rendered	11,862
Regattas patrolled	4,731
Lives saved	527

It is clear from the above that there is a stringent assessment of lives saved and that not every body picked out of the water is added to the total automatically. The figures compare with the total search and rescue details for the whole regular US Coast Guard force with 50,000 distress calls answered and 3,000 lives saved. Two-thirds of all USCG search and rescue operations resulted from requests for assistance from privately owned vessels. Enrolled Auxiliaries are entitled to wear a smart uniform when on duty and have their own officers ranging from national commodore to flotilla staff officer. A volunteer force of this magnitude, committed to dealing with people prone to highly individualistic temperaments and a frequently unpredictable element like the sea, must surely have proved its worth over the years to compensate for the administrative headaches it must produce for the Coast Guard executive.

In countries where the rescue service is a voluntary one, participation by the yachting and boating public tends to be an individual matter and to a large extent confined to subscriptions and donations. Many keen amateur seamen do join lifeboat crews, some becoming coxswain of their boat but group participation on the operational side, such as by a yacht club, is almost if not quite unknown. There are a number of small private rescue organisations but most of these operate quite independently and in Britain it is doubtful whether the RNLI views them with any great enthusiasm. This is not to decry the motives or ability of keen rescue teams but they do tend to complicate matters and can cause a certain amount of dissatisfaction amongst lifeboat crews. In the USA, two-thirds of the calls for assistance came from pleasure craft. In Britain the RNLI reported that in 1971 the proportion was a little more than half. It is clear that the yachting and boating public have a vested interest in sea safety.

One interesting suggestion came from the Canadian Coast Guard, to the effect that there appear to be signs of a declining standard of self-reliance among seamen generally. If this proves to be correct, it may possibly be due to increasing instrumentation, mechanisation and even domestication of ships, with much shorter tours of duty and much longer shore leave. In what way this declining standard was manifested was not disclosed but presumably there had been calls for assistance which in the opinion of the Coast Guard were not justified.

Assessment of facilities

The RNLI, and no doubt all sea rescue organisations, keep every lifeboat station constantly under review in order to assess their effectiveness. In some cases, the necessity for their continued existence must also be considered. With escalating costs and the possible requirement for new stations, this is clearly of great importance but it is never easy to put into practice a decision to close a station. Disasters never give warning of their approach and the closure of a lifeboat station which has done no effective work for years could easily be followed by a major wreck on the very spot.

In order to consider briefly the development of lifeboats and rescue craft now and in the future, it would be as well to determine the types of casualties for which they must cater. These may be conveniently divided into four main classes, although the RNLI in its annual report lists no less than seventeen categories. Here are the four:

1 Off a beach and close inshore, such as bathing, boating, small inflatables, people marooned on rocks and cliffs and the like;
2 Close offshore, and likely to be power boats, sailing craft and small vessels generally;
3 Offshore, possibly some distance; larger vessels, drilling rigs, lightships, aircraft;
4 Ambulance work and other miscellaneous acts of mercy.

The inflatable or other type of fast inshore lifeboat is generally suitable to deal with classes 1 and 2, but many factors are involved and there can always be exceptions. Classes 3 and 4 call for a conventional lifeboat or rescue cruiser and can also pose some problems in the matter of suitability. There is always the possibility that any rescue problem may be solved by helicopters, but it must not be taken for granted that they are infallible. In some weather conditions their use is questionable – in fog or thick mist for instance.

Naturally, there must be basic requirements and acknowledged priorities in the design of a lifeboat. An arbitrary selection might be:

Seaworthiness
Ability to work in shallow, broken water
Adequate protection for crew
Suitable speed
Proper navigational equipment
Ability to tow
Economy in prime cost and maintenance.

Opinions on the items and their order will probably vary. Self-righting ability has not been listed separately but may be taken as included in seaworthiness if experience eventually proves that it is essential. Of the requirements listed, the most flexible and debatable is speed.

The question of speed in sea rescue work is an extremely complex one. The general opinion is naturally that as rescue is often a matter of life and death, speed is vital. In fact, a careful analysis of lifeboat services shows that this is rarely the case. If a swimmer is reported in difficulties, there is no doubt that immediate assistance is necessary as people can drown very quickly. But the hard fact is that in most drowning fatalities the victim is often dead before help is summoned. People on the spot do their utmost to carry out a rescue and it is usually only when it is clear that they have failed that the lifeboat or helicopter is brought into it. Nevertheless, speed is essential in such cases and will continue to be so, however rare a successful outcome. A capsized dinghy and other small boat or inflatable casualties do not often have the same urgency providing the victim hangs on to his craft. Though he may be unconscious from a blow on the head or trapped by some gear and need the swiftest possible help.

For casualties of this sort, the inshore lifeboat is ideal. With over 100 ILB's carefully sited round the coast of Britain at points of maximum sea sport activity, the chances of a quick rescue are good, but it is still possible for accidents to happen a long way from immediate aid; and of course it is necessary for someone to sight the casualty and send for assistance. The quieter the spot, the less likely this is to happen.

One instance of rescue in the nick of time occurred at Rhyl in North Wales some years ago. Two boys aged about seven and ten had drifted out to sea in a rubber dinghy. The coxswain of the lifeboat from his local knowledge was able to make a good estimate of the probable direction of drift and just as it was growing dusk the head of one of the boys was sighted, just clear of the water. As the lifeboat came up the crew found the elder boy standing on a sandbank which the rising tide had submerged. In his arms he was holding the younger boy with his mouth just above water. In a matter of minutes they would both have been drowned. Here was a case where every minute counted and one which understandably gave tremendous satisfaction to the Rhyl lifeboatmen.

In considering speed, the possible use of hovercraft for rescue work has been considered and is no doubt being kept under review by the world's lifeboat organisations. The hovercraft would appear to have considerable possibilities in places where there are large areas of swamp, sandbanks or mudbanks (see chapter three – Canada).

That speed has many advantages is undeniable. Not only does it cut down the time taken to reach a casualty but it also increases the area which one boat can cover effectively, thereby decreasing the number of boats required. Speed in a conventional lifeboat is most likely to be necessary when dealing with a ditched aircraft and with drilling rigs. The first for obvious reasons and the other because of the distances usually involved. Drilling rigs do not lend themselves to rescue from the sea because of their construction and are likely to be best evacuated by helicopter. For example, in 1971 RNLI lifeboats carried out 21 services to aircraft and 6 to drilling rigs. These compare with no less than 1,628 services to pleasure craft of all kinds. In general, it would appear that there is a more obvious and more constant need for speed with ILBs because of the type of casualty they deal with. With the larger boats operating offshore it would seem that speed is desirable but not very often a vital necessity.

A lifeboat's varied functions

It is necessary that a lifeboat should be able to deal with any type of casualty and in any weather conditions, with some efficiency. There is every indication that over the years they have performed extremely well and dealt with a large range of less predictable accidents. In the remote parts of a country, ambulance work often forms one of the most important functions of a lifeboat. They take doctors out to sick people in ships and on remote islands and bring patients back to hospital. It was reported by one station whose lifeboat had brought a woman with a broken thigh through 40 miles of gale-lashed seas that '– the patient had a comfortable trip'! And more than one lifeboat, taking a maternity case to the mainland, has had to turn the tiny cabin into a labour ward. Possibly the most traumatic experience was that of the Barra island lifeboat in the Outer Hebrides, off the western coast of Scotland. They made the long trip out to the remote island of St Kilda in order to take a seaman from a Spanish trawler to hospital, as he was dangerously ill. The man was delirious and had to be attended throughout the long journey home. The lifeboat was met by a doctor on arrival and the Spaniard was found to be suffering from typhoid. The lifeboat crew were informed that they could not come ashore until they had been inoculated. It is said that tired as they were, they accepted the verdict stoically.

Almost certainly one of the most fearful hazards at sea is

that of fire. A ship is particularly vulnerable, and in spite of modern fire-fighting methods and equipment, many vessels have been lost by fire in recent years. An oil tanker fire, with hundreds of tons of burning oil spreading across the sea, presents a ghastly rescue problem and one with which the majority of rescue craft are probably ill-equipped to deal.

For example, only a small number of RNLI lifeboats are equipped to deal with fires in casualties and this only on a small scale. None have special fire protection for the crew and boat itself other than the usual extinguishers. A number of foreign lifeboats are fitted with water-spraying devices but the effectiveness of at least some of these is in doubt as they are said to generate steam, which causes more injuries than the fire itself.

At the 1967 International Lifeboat Conference in Dinard,

Bridlington lifeboat on service in heavy seas.

the Japanese delegation produced a most interesting and detailed paper on an experimental ship's lifeboat, designed to allow the crew of a tanker to escape from a burning vessel and through burning oil on the surface of the sea. They also gave details of the destruction by fire of the 35,355 ton Norwegian tanker *Heim Vard* at a port in Hokkaido in 1965. This resulted in the loss of ten lives and much damage to other vessels and property and it took nearly a month to get the fire under control.

All major ports and installations are equipped for fighting oil fires afloat and it is unlikely that lifeboats would become immediately involved. A fire at sea, possibly due to a collision, might be another matter and must be a problem that is causing some concern to rescue organisations. It is undoubtedly one of the most important subjects for investigation and co-operation on an international plane.

Costs

For most rescue organisations, and this includes even those that are controlled by government departments, money is an ever present problem. More sophisticated craft and equipment are increasing the ever escalating costs. How long the voluntary institutions will be able to cope with this situation must be a question that is exercising the minds of those responsible. Some idea of what is involved may be obtained from the fact that the cost of running the RNLI in 1946 was about £800,000 compared with £5,500,000 in 1975. In fact, this is only about in proportion to the drop in purchasing power of the pound sterling and fortunately not in proportion to the increased number of calls for assistance. It says a lot for the efficient management of the RNLI.

The cost of air search-and-rescue of surface craft has been mentioned but owing to the fact that service aircraft are employed it is difficult to determine the actual sums involved. A certain amount can be written off as useful training but some operations must have cost the taxpayer £20,000 or more and there have been significant suggestions in official circles that the owner of the casualty should be made to bear his share.

How does it happen that in a number of countries the whole of the lifeboat service is financed by voluntary donations and in many others a substantial part of the money required is raised in this way? The sea and seamen have always had a romantic appeal and seafaring has always been a dangerous occupation, but this hardly gives a reason in depth for the fact that even in the hardest times people continue to subscribe. That brave men have always volunteered to carry out the hazardous work of rescue is perhaps the real reason that the various governments have been reluctant to assume the responsibility, and why the general public have so enthusiastically supported a voluntary service.

So we find that sea rescue, a basically simple thing, is becoming more and more sophisticated and expensive. The suggestion that it must be a responsibility of the State is understandable but not necessarily logical since the difficulties, dangers and discomfort often involved are not easily equated in terms of authority or finance. The duties are likely to be most readily undertaken by volunteers and in times of rapidly changing values the courage and humanity of the men of the rescue services still shine like a good deed in a naughty world.

APPENDIX

LIST OF LIFEBOAT ASSOCIATIONS AND SEA RESCUE ORGANISATIONS

COUNTRY	ORGANISATION
Australia	Queenscliff Lifeboat Service* (Victoria Ports and Harbours Division)
Belgium	Administration de la Marine et de la Navigation Interieure*
Bermuda	The Bermuda Search and Rescue Institute
Bahamas	Bahamas Air Sea Rescue Association*
Canada	Canadian Coast Guard*
Chile	Cuerpo de Voluntarios de los Botes Salvavidas de Valparaiso*
Denmark	Bestyreren af Redningsvaesenet
Faroe Islands	Bjargingarfelag Föroya*
Finland	Åland Life-Boat Society* and Suomen Meripelastusseura*
France	Société Nationale de Sauvetage en Mer*
Germany (West)	Deutsche Gesellschaft zür Rettung Schiffbruchiger*
(East)	Seefahrtsamt der Deutşchen Republik*
Guatemala	Ministro de Defensa Nacional
Iceland	Slysavarnahusinu Grandagardi*
India	Department of Lighthouses and Lightships
Italy	Capitanerie di Porto
Japan	Nippon Suinan Kyusaikai* and Maritime Safety Agency*
Netherlands	Koninklijke Zuid-Hollandandsche Maatschappij tot Redding van

	Schippbreukelingen* and Koninklijke Noord-En Zuid-Hollandsche Redding Maatschappij*
New Zealand	Sumner Life-Boat Institution Inc.* and Wellington Sea-Rescue Service WRC.
Norway	Norsk Selskab til Skibbrudnes Redning*
Poland	Polskie Ratownictwo Okretowe*
Portugal	Instituto de Socorros a Náufragos*
South Africa	National Sea Rescue Institute of South Africa*
Spain	Cruz Roja del Mar*
Sweden	Svenska Sällskapet för Räddning af Skeppsbrutne*
Switzerland	Société International de Sauvetage du Leman*
Turkey	Denizcilik Bankasi TAO
United Kingdom and Ireland	Royal National Lifeboat Institution*
Uruguay	Associacion Honoraria de Salvamentos Maritimos y Fluviales*
USA	United States Coast Guard*
USSR	Ministry of Merchant Marine*

* Organisations registered with the International Lifeboat Conference at the ILC's permanent base in the RNLI Head Office, West Quay Road, Poole, Dorset BH15 1HZ, England.

INDEX

INDEX

Names of vessels are in *italic*.
Names of overseas organisations and government departments are
followed by the name of the country in parentheses, where this
is not obvious from the title.